WONDERS
—OF THE—
ANCIENT WORLD

WONDERS
OF THE
ANCIENT WORLD

Charles Walker

CRESCENT BOOKS
New York

©Orbis Publishing Limited, London MCMLXXX
First English edition of this book published by
Orbis Publishing Limited, London MCMLXXX
All rights reserved.
This edition is published by Crescent Books, a division of
Crown Publishers, Inc.
a b c d e f g h
Printed in Czechoslovakia

Library of Congress Cataloging in Publication Data
Walker, Charles
   Wonders of the ancient world.

   Bibliography: p.
   Includes index.
   1. Curiosities and wonders. I. Title.
AG243.K44   1980   722   80-65756
ISBN 0-517-318253
   50130

Page 1 Gold burial mask from Mycenae
Title page Ruins of the Apadana, Persepolis

Contents

Nothing beside remains. Round the decay
Of that colossal wreck, boundless and bare
The lone and level sands stretch far away.
Percy Bysshe Shelley, 'Ozymandias'

When we build, let us think that we build
    for ever.
John Ruskin, *The Seven Lamps of Architecture*

The Seven Wonders of the Ancient World

So long is the journey which must be made in order to see the seven wonders of the world, that you find yourself 'exhausted by lengthy wanderings over the Earth's surface, and growing tired from the efforts of these journeys, you finally fulfil your heart's desire only when life is ebbing away, leaving you weak through the weight of the years'. So wrote Philon of Byzantium, somewhat lugubriously, as though there were no joy in travelling, in his commentary on the seven wonders of his day. But since those ancient times, the world has shrunk, and time has been telescoped by just one of the many wonders of the modern world – jet travel.

Only one of the wonders listed by Philon is still in existence, and a flight to Cairo, followed by a short taxi ride (or, should you seek to enter into the spirit of the thing, a rather longer ride on a camel) will take you to the very ancient pyramids which were old even when Philon wrote, and which have indeed been the wonder of the world since man began records of what amazed him. There is none of Philon's despairing weariness in such a tourist trip, and it may well teach the lesson that time is money. For the cost of the jet and the taxi or camel, you will have saved many days, and possibly much blood and tears.

Now that travel is quicker and less dangerous, and, incidentally, far less romantic, the world has been found to contain many more than the seven ancient wonders, and it is with comparative ease that almost two score have been selected for this book, nearly all of which compete at least on equal terms with those of the ancient world. Among these are the temple at Pagan, which is the biggest in the world; the temple-pyramid at Teotihuacan, which covers an area larger than the Great Pyramid in Egypt; the Pantheon of ancient and modern Rome, which is the most beautifully preserved of all ancient buildings; and the Great Wall of China, which modern photographic techniques have shown to be visible even from the moon. There are indeed so many miracles of engineering and design available to us these days that it would have been possible to select yet another forty ancient buildings or sites without even mentioning those listed here, and still we would not have exhausted the real miracles of man's art, energy and enterprise.

The fact is that there are hundreds of miracles on the earth, and perhaps a reasonably travelled person could now name at least fifty wonders comparable to the original seven, even without escaping from the confines accepted as belonging to the ancient world. There must have been just as many in ancient times, contemporaneous with the reign of Alexander the Great, when such lists were first compiled. And, therefore, the question is why were there only seven wonders listed in the first place?

The answer is comparatively simple, if somewhat foreign to our understanding. It lies in the fact that the number seven was itself a holy number. We have inherited the seven wonders for the same reason that we have inherited a seven-day week – because, according to the ancients, there are seven planets, and because these were governed by seven angelic beings, seven gods, and seven evil demons. There were seven deadly sins, and seven great virtues, and for the same reason there were seven sleepers in Ephesus. When the late medieval magicians wrote their tracts on numbers, they always gave precedence to the number seven, to the 'holy number', for within its compass were said to lie the secrets of the universe, to a point where it was believed that any man who could piece together the mysteries of seven and three would attain all human knowledge!

This is why there were seven wonders listed in the ancient world – not because there were only seven great marvels!

And so, what are the wonders listed by Philon? In brief they consist of the Pyramids of Egypt, the Hanging Gardens in Babylon, the Statue of Zeus in Olympia, the Temple of Artemis at Ephesus, the Mausoleum at Halicarnassus, the Colossus of Rhodes, and, finally, the Lighthouse at Alexandria.

If we discount the pyramids, which could scarcely be left out of any such list, then we find that all these were built within a few centuries of the rule of Alexander the Great, and they all existed in the countries in which Alexander was victorious. This would suggest that this ancient list was in some way concerned with applauding the magnificence of this great Macedonian, or providing a sort of advertising campaign for the Greek nation.

Such a theory would in fact be supported by a glance into other later 'lists' of the seven wonders; lists which were adopted by commentators and historians with interests in adulating things other than those of the Greek nation. For example, there is an old list of the post-Christian era, said to have been promulgated by Gregory of Tours in the sixth century, which shows some knowledge of such ancient authorities as Herodotus. This substitutes for the Hanging Gardens the Walls of Babylon, and introduces as wonders Noah's Ark, along with Solomon's Temple, both of which advertise the Christian view of the world.

Philon's list is the most ancient known, and one of the clues to the date it was compiled is found in the list itself. Since he names as one of the wonders the Statue f Helios at Rhodes, we must presume that the list was not constructed until after 290 BC, when this was erected. We know, however, that within sixty-three years an earthquake had thrown this colossus down, and we may therefore reasonably suspect that, since the Helios described by Philon is said to be still standing, the seven wonders he gives us were compiled around that time. The emphasis on Greek art and the genius of the Greek artist Phidias would suggest also a Greek origin for the list. The Pyramids would be regarded as marking one boundary of the civilized world (that is, the world under the control of Alexandrian Greece), while the inclusion of Babylon, with its walls and gardens, would mark the tragic end of the Persian Empire which had dared to confront the might of Greece.

It is evident, therefore, that the list which we have inherited of the seven wonders is a fragment of ancient advertising. There are many such lists, with different 'products' in mind, some of which even broke the magic number seven to produce larger numbers of wonders, perhaps to involve some boasting of personal travels and knowledge. In his study of the seven wonders, the modern writer Martin Ashley gives four unorthodox early lists, and it is gratifying to note that two sites are mentioned which are included within the present text – the Baths of Caracalla and the Colosseum in Rome. Needless to say, this particular list, derived from an obscure Spaniard who chose to live in Rome, is directed towards advertising Roman greatness, rather than Greek, with the result that only one of the ancient Grecian wonders is included.

In order to avoid being caught in the sharp brambles which are thick on each side of the path of any historian who chooses to march into the past, we may sensibly remain with the classical list of the seven wonders, which is by now hallowed by both tradition and age. It is certainly worth attempting a description of these seven wonders, if only to see why they should have been considered so remarkable, so worthy of inclusion in so short a list, no matter what individual or culture they were designed to eulogize.

Before examining in more detail these seven traditional wonders, it is as well to observe that the engravings made by the Dutch artist Heemskerck in the sixteenth century, used to illustrate this section of the book, are by no means intended to give an idea of the actual wonders themselves – far from it! Heemskerck had little evidence on which to build his picture of these ancient constructions. Like other artists before and since, he depicts the past much in the form of his own time, and his engravings show how an age is inclined to see the past in its own image. Note, for example, the sixteenth-century version of the Temple of Artemis at Ephesus: it looks something like a Rococo nightmare of Borromini, rather than expressive of Greek architecture at its finest. This is a good example to take, because we are more fortunate than Heemskerck, as the recent discovery of the actual foundations of the archaic temple at Ephesus has enabled historians to make fairly accurate assess-

To us today a somewhat humorous 'reconstruction' of the Pyramids by an artist who clearly never saw them, but had to rely on hearsay. From a sixteenth-century engraving by Maarten van Heemskerck (1498–1574).

PIRAMIDES ÆGYPTI.

ments of what the temple looked like in its original form. In view of the extensive literature and topographical records a more surprising example of Heemskerck's distortion is his version of the pyramids, which are here reduced to fanciful columns almost libellous of Egyptian fame.

The pyramids were an obvious choice for any ancient list, for they are still a wonder in this modern world, which is a little jaded with wonders both ancient and modern. We must presume that of the seventy known pyramids in Egypt, it was the group at Giza, near Cairo, which Philon had in mind. It is probable that he was referring to this group, which includes the Great Pyramid, the oldest according to the guesswork of archaeologists, for Philon talks of the pyramids 'at Memphis' which is near enough to Giza, but also not very far from Saqqarah. He describes them as

BABYLONIS MVRI.

1572

The hanging gardens of Babylon, looking something like a roof-garden, are to the right. Heemskerck was more interested in the city walls, which he lists as the second of the seven ancient wonders.

buildings 'beyond the strength of men, as is their description beyond belief', and pictures them as mountains placed on mountains, wondering then, as we wonder now, how such masses could have been raised above the earth and sands.

We must remember that if Philon saw the pyramids at all, then he saw the Cairo group in their pristine covering before the outer layer of white stone was removed to build the mosques in Cairo. This facing would have glowed in the sun, especially in the rising and setting of that Egyptian Ra, when they would have appeared to burn red in the reflected rays – reminding us that one (though dubious) etymology of the word 'pyramid' has been traced to the Greek word for 'fire'.

The one indication which would persuade me that Philon actually visited the pyramids is his comment that in order to really appreciate them you have to climb them. Climbing the pyramids is forbidden these days, and when I did it some years ago, it was at risk of life and limb, not merely from the danger of the powdered stone which precludes any sureness of foot, but from the threats of the guides who do not really care whether you climb them or not, provided you give them *baksheesh* for doing either.

Philon's summary of the effect of the pyramids encapsulates the quality of all great works of art: 'for by works of this kind, either men rise up to the gods, or the gods themselves come down to man'. The perfect theory of art,

and one obviously applicable to many of the sites which will be examined in this book.

With the second wonder, the Hanging Gardens of Babylon, we enter a region of the world known to the bitter Greek and Hebrew nations alike. The Greek historian Herodotus describes in some detail the walls of this extraordinary city of Babylon, but makes no mention of the hanging gardens. From other sources we must take it that these were a series of verdant and colourful terraces, fed by water ducted from the Euphrates. Until this present century few writers could explain why these gardens should have been ascribed to the 'legendary' Queen Semiramis, when it was well known that the building of Babylon had been undertaken by Nebuchadnezzar. Until 1909, when a fallen column was found describing Semiramis as 'ruler of the world of Assyria, and the Four Quarters of the world', it was believed that Philon and the other major authority, Diodorus of Sicily, had been inventing this queen. Now it is generally accepted that she was indeed at one time queen of Babylon, and wife of Ninus, even though she was later transformed into a mythical figure and goddess. Perhaps, on this evidence, it might be reasonable to suppose that the ancients were right in ascribing the gardens to her in the first place.

Certainly Philon writes of this queen as though she were an historical figure. He also reports that the garden ran around the entire walls of Babylon, which would make it literally miles in length. It is possible, however, that Philon is trying to weld together the two wonders of which travellers to Babylon speak, for we are told of walls which are 50 cubits high, and 360 stadia wide, so that four chariots might drive along them at the same time, a description which is to be found in several ancient sources.

Almost all the so-called reconstructions of the gardens are based on the description given by Diodorus of Sicily, a commentator otherwise well known for his inventions. He describes the gardens as though they were a huge theatre some 30 metres (100 feet) square, built in high tiers, the upper vault of which was 22·5 metres (75 feet) from the ground. However, one might consider these rather disappointing credentials for an ancient wonder and Diodorus may have his facts wrong, as he so often does.

The ancients rarely attempt to explain how the gardens were watered. A few speak of 'screws' and 'mechanical devices', but this was a time when manpower was cheap, being provided by slaves, and it would not be unusual for the slave owner to expect his property to carry water all day and night if necessary. This could be done using flights of stairs, carefully hidden to avoid spoiling the view of the gardens. However, when the archaeologist Robert Koldewey excavated the site of Babylon towards the end of the last century, he discovered a deep well quite unlike any other in the ancient world, and from the construction of this he deduced that water had been drawn by means of a chain pump. His own reconstruction of the gardens is based on the assumption that such a pump had been used, and incorporated a stone vault which he found nearby. Curiously enough, his reconstruction looks something like a theatre!

The third wonder is the statue of Zeus, which was made by Phidias for the temple at Olympia. This was the same Phidias who gave us the statue of Athena and the friezes of the Acropolis in Athens, and this naturally leads us to ask why the Acropolis itself, or indeed the much-praised Athena within the Parthenon there, was not included in the original list of wonders.

This Zeus was certainly very different from the sixteenth-century image drawn by Heemskerck, which not only lacks dignity, but also has some of the recorded symbolism wrong. Incidentally, the figures twisting so suggestively in the foreground of this print are not indulging in pagan sexual licence, as one might think, but are wrestling, which serves as a reminder that Olympia was the site of the ancient Olympic Games.

The great temple in the sacred grove of Olympia which housed Phidias's massive statue was filled almost to its 18-metre (50-foot) roof by this figure. Its flesh parts were made from ivory over a stone or wooden core, and the drapery and accoutrements were made from gold set with precious stones. In his right hand Zeus was said to hold an ivory and gold statue of Victory, and in his left the eagle-mounted sceptre.

Phidias has been much praised by whole generations of art historians who have never seen a trace of his original works. Only a few poor copies of his art have survived, though quite unhelpful mould-forms have been

found of his famous Zeus. The frieze on the Parthenon, which now graces the British Museum in London, was carved within the studio he controlled, but there is little agreement among historians as to whether his 'divine hand' was in the work. Philon had presumably seen at least the Olympian Zeus, if not the Athena at the Parthenon, for he speaks of 'the hands of Phidias, which alone of humans have satisfied the gods'. And he attempts a remarkable literary conceit when he imagines that nature created the African elephant in order to provide Phidias with ivory to work his wonders of carving! Sadly, we learn little about the statue itself from this source, however, presumably because it is so well known to his readers that no detailed description was felt to be needed.

Phidias's Zeus led to his being accounted divine, but his Athena served as an excuse for his being thrown into prison. When his great

supporter and client Pericles fell into disfavour with the Athenians, Phidias was accused of keeping some of the gold intended for Athena for his own purposes. He soon cleared himself of this charge, but was in spite of this still thrown into prison on the grounds of impiety, for he had introduced human portraits on the shield of his goddess!

The statue of Zeus was accounted more than a 'wonder', it became almost an educational necessity, and the philosopher Epictetus maintained at the beginning of the second century, when the statue still stood in Olympia, that it was a tragedy for someone to die without having seen it. Many of those who saw the figure insisted that it was more than merely a work of art, but was actually the body into which Zeus himself would incarnate!

For once, this wonder was not destroyed by man. It was removed from Olympia by the

The statue of Zeus at Olympia, as visualized by Heemskerck. The wrestling figures in the foreground are there to remind us that this was the site of the ancient Olympic Games.

Christian Emperor Theodosius I to Constantinople, 'the second Rome', and it was destroyed there in an enormous conflagration in AD 475. We have no real conception of what the figure looked like; without exception, all the reconstructions I know are quite hideous.

The Colossus of Rhodes was said to have been made by Chares of Lindus. It was a statue on a scale approaching that of the modern Statue of Liberty in New York, and was indeed one of the main inspirations for this modern work, erected in 1896 to commemorate the French and American revolutions. The ancient colossus took twelve years to build, from 292 to 280 BC, and it stood for only a few years before it was felled by an earthquake in 224 BC.

It was said to be upwards of 32 metres (105 feet) tall, a Helios Sun-god, 'a likeness of the sun' as Philon calls it. He tells how it was made from stones joined together on the inside with iron bolts (a fairly common technique in ancient building), the entire statue being coated in plates of bronze. It was then placed upon a pure white marble block, almost as high as the statue itself. The difficulty of raising this huge form on to a high block is described by Philon, who insists that some miraculous force 'like that used in the building of the temples of the gods' was used, so that it was as though the figure lifted of its own accord.

This Helios colossus is often pictured astride two pedestals, sometimes even with boats passing beneath its legs into the harbour, as for example in the engraving by Heemskerck. This is of course entirely imaginative, and, in terms of the sculptural and building techniques of the ancients, quite impossible. The most reasonable reconstruction is that made by Sir Herbert Maryon,

Heemskerck's reconstruction of the colossus at Rhodes. In common with many other artists, Heemskerck depicts the colossus straddling the entrance to the harbour, although modern archaeologists state that this would have been impossible. Also, the head would have been much larger in proportion to the human beings than it is shown in the foreground to this engraving.

COLOSSVS SOLIS.

DIANÆ EPHESIÆ TEMPLVM

based on the known Grecian style and
methods of the period. This shows the statue
with a rayed nimbus around his head, shield-
ing his eyes as though looking over to the
rising (or setting) sun. In his left hand he
trails a cloak, but is otherwise naked. This
cloak of bronze would have been a structural
device to aid the stability of the colossus, for
it would have given the figure a secure tripod
rest to the pedestal, rather than the less
secure balance of only two feet.

Records show that, like many ancient
statues in Egypt, the fallen Helios remained
prone where it had fallen in the earthquake
until AD 672, when it was sold by a Muslim
general for scrap.

Virtually every trace of the seven wonders
(the pyramids being excepted, as usual) has
disappeared. The bronze of the Helios
colossus was melted down, the Phidias Zeus

was destroyed in a fire, and so on. With the
fifth great ancient wonder, however, which
was also considered to be 'lost' to the world,
we have recently witnessed a kind of miracle
of resurrection. As a result of archaeological
research and discoveries, not only has it been
possible to reconstruct almost every detail of
the original form of the Temple of Artemis at
Ephesus, but some of the original archaic
remains are even to be seen in the British
Museum in London.

The original temple was said to have been
designed by Cherisphron in the sixth century,
but it was burned down two centuries later.
The rebuilt temple, constructed on the same
ground plan, stood for nearly five centuries
until the Goths sacked Ephesus in AD 262.
For many centuries that was believed to be
the whole patchy history of this temple.

After exhaustive and exhausting digging

last century, the archaeologist J. T. Wood, from the British Museum, succeeded in his mission to find the temple remains. Later surveys revealed signs of the ancient foundations of the archaic temple, along with thousands of small golden votive offerings. As a result of these discoveries, we may speculate more usefully, and with some degree of certainty, about the form of the first temple. An excellent reconstruction has been published in Banister Fletcher's *A History of Architecture,* and is worth examination.

The wife of King Mausolus, Queen Artemisia – who is not to be confused with Artemisia I, the woman who was present with Xerxes at the battle of Salamis – built the sixth wonder of the world as a token of her love for her husband. This was later called the Mausoleum, a specific name which was eventually applied to all such monuments on a large scale intended to house the dead. This Mausoleum was said to have been designed by Pythius, with sculptural decorations by almost legendary artists such as Scopas and Praxiteles, whose work, like that of Phidias, is known only by reputation (though it is claimed with some reason that one of the sculpted heads now kept in Boston in the USA, is actually from the school of the latter Greek).

The Mausoleum was built at Halicarnassus, the modern Bodrum, a city of Asia Minor on the south-west coast of Caria, opposite the island of Kos. As with so many of the wonders, our knowledge of it, as indeed of Halicarnassus itself, is derived mainly from Philon, but also from the Roman Vitruvius, who had considerable influence on the Italian Renaissance when some of his writings were rediscovered. Vitruvius writes also of other wonders at this place – for example, of a concealed harbour there, known only to the king – but he does mention that the Mausoleum is one of the seven wonders of the world.

Since the Mausoleum was set halfway up the hill, in the middle of a broad street or processional, it would have been a familiar landmark to travellers and voyagers by sea. There are many descriptions of it, from which a variety of reconstructions have been made.

Pliny gives a fairly detailed account of the building, and we have every reason for supposing that this Roman had actually visited Halicarnassus. He tells us that the length of the façade and sides was 132 metres (440 feet), and that it was enclosed by thirty-six columns. The east side was said to have been carved by Scopas, the north by Bryaxis, the south by Timotheos, the west by Leochares. At the summit was a *quadriga* (a four-horse chariot) made by Pythius, which Pliny said brought the height of the entire building to 42 metres (140 feet). It is recorded that even though Queen Artemisia died before the work was completed in 352 BC, the sculptors continued their tasks in the full knowledge that their work would remain a symbol of their own artistic glory.

In 1856, Sir Charles Newton managed to locate the site of the destroyed Mausoleum, and was able to put on record the precise dimensions. These correspond fairly closely to the figures given by Pliny. From this certain knowledge, and from what we know of the mathematical ratios used by Greek architects of that period, it has been possible to reconstruct something of the likely appearance of the building. Such reconstructions give a podium, colonnade and roof-pyramid in the ratio of 3:3:3, surmounted by a quadriga one-ninth of the total height.

The Mausoleum was ruined first in an earthquake, round about AD 1400, but it survived in this form until 1522. The Knights of St John (the Hospitaller), who had captured the area in 1402, then obtained special dispensation from Pope Gregory XII to use the ancient stones of the Greeks in order to build a much-needed fortress. As a result, by 1522 the Mausoleum had been completely dismantled, even though it was in that year that the Knights themselves, after a seven-month siege on the island of Rhodes, were overwhelmed by the invading Ottomans.

It is frequently claimed, even in academic works which should know better, that the two statues in the British Museum, of 'Mausolus' and 'Artemisia' originally stood in the quadriga which surmounted the Mausoleum. This is entirely a matter of speculation, and there is no proof that the statues even represent the pair at all. On the other hand, a few of the friezes within the Museum, weathered and partly destroyed as they are, certainly did belong to the original building, for they were sent to London by Lord Canning, who found them inset in the walls of the castle built by the Knights of St John.

In the first century before Christ, the Greek geographer Strabo left a description of the

MAVSOLÆVM.

Heemskerck's concept of what the Mausoleum of Artemisia at Halicarnassus must have looked like.

seventh wonder of the ancient world, the Pharos, or lighthouse, at Alexandria, in which he says that it is 'admirably constructed of white marble, with many storeys . . . built by Sostratos of Cnidos for the safety of sailors'. With this seventh wonder, located at the entrance to an Egyptian harbour (though built by a Greek) we have completed a full circle, and as Ashley says, 'Egypt lays claim to both the alpha and the omega of the Wonders'.

As the name indicates, and was indeed intended to proclaim, the city which this lighthouse served was founded by Alexander the Great. Within a few decades (from 332 BC), he built the most important city in the entire Mediterranean on the ruins of a tiny fishing village. As travellers are still allowed to dream, I like to think that Alexander himself arranged for the construction of this lighthouse as a sort of external symbol of

Greek culture. The fire and smoke from its tall tower would guide men in the external material world, while the enormous library in this same city (the finest library known to the world) would light their way in the inner spiritual world. The knowledge of the books would be seen for ever, and would spread across the globe, such is the power of the invisible realm of ideas. Unfortunately, the library declined and was accidentally destroyed in the late third century A.D.

However, my speculation is not strictly speaking based on historical fact, for there is unfortunately no evidence that Alexander ordered the lighthouse, and we are told that it was built by the architect Sostratos around 271 BC, in the reign of Ptolemy Philadelphus. Apparently, the lighthouse could be seen 56 kilometres (35 miles) out to sea, its long column of smoke by day, and its flames by night.

The exact height of the Pharos is not known, though it was probably about 138 metres (460 feet) high. Excluding the Great Pyramid, the Pharos was the tallest single building of antiquity. It was placed upon a 6-metre (20-foot) high masonry platform, some 108 metres (360 feet) square, with a base of 30 metres (100 feet), the inner structure containing as many rooms as those commentators who wrote about it guessed was possible – estimates vary from 50 to 300. There was said to be a spiral internal ramp (placed by Heemskerck on the outside) that facilitated the lifting of fuel to a certain level, from where it was then lifted by tackle to the domed shelter, which was said to contain a large statue of the sea-god Poseidon. There was supposed to be within the upper dome a convex mirror, or mirrors, of polished bronze to reflect the sun's rays on to enemy ships – but one feels instinctively that this belief is merely romantic speculation.

This lighthouse almost enters recorded modern history. It appears to have functioned for nearly a thousand years, in more or less its original state. However, when the lantern collapsed in AD 700, Arabs, who had by then overrun the area, put in its place a huge fire-brazier, and this continued in use for about four centuries. The earthquake of 1375, which is supposed to have brought down the lighthouse, was in fact merely putting a finishing touch to the work done by man. By 1477 the Sultan Quit Bei decided to build a castle on the site of the lighthouse, and much of the original masonry was used in this scheme.

Thus passed from the material stream of things the last of the six great wonders, leaving only the pyramids standing serene, against their backcloth of eternal blue skies.

Heemskerck's imaginative version of the Pharos, or Lighthouse, at Alexandria.

EGYPT

The Sphinx at Giza, near Cairo, carved from the living rock. The Great Pyramid can be seen in the background.

The Pyramids

As we approach the three large pyramids at Giza (the last remains of the seven ancient wonders), perhaps swaying uncomfortably on the back of a camel, we may at first be a little disappointed. The structures in the distance are familiar, for they remind us of a hundred photographs we have seen in books and magazines; they are no doubt romantic against that blue Egyptian sky, but they are only pyramids of stone. But then, as we reach the straight base of stones, they begin to encircle us, so that the normal sense of scale values crumbles. Against such massive forms, the human being is dwarfed in space, and, glimpsing eternity in the mass before him, he feels also contracted in time. It is as though these stones distort human history itself. There is something so superhuman in their construction that it would be easy to credit the ancient legends that they were built by giants or gods, or carried here by magicians using the anti-gravitational forces once known to the priests of the fabled lost continent of Atlantis.

If not actually made by gods, they were certainly intended to serve them, for they were constructed by a people for whom the division between the living and the dead was more nebulous than is generally believed nowadays. The pyramids and tombs around them, with the complex of temples, embalming chambers, and the Sphinx, were built to serve the god-king pharaoh and his large retinue of priests. They were reputed to be adepts in the Mysteries, with an occult power over the two worlds of the living and the dead, as comfortable in this world as in the Amenti afterworld which they saw all around them.

These three pyramids are said to have been built by the Pharaohs Cheops, Chephren and Mycerinus, probably over five thousand years ago. The largest is the 'Great Pyramid' of Cheops which consists of an almost solid mass of masonry (except for the space taken up by the internal chambers and passages) in a bulk of some 2·3 million cu. metres (85 million cu. feet). An idea of this vastness may be conveyed by imagining the Empire State Building in New York thirty times higher than it now stands – that is with 2550 storeys – for this would be about the equivalent bulk of masonry. Not surprisingly, the Great Pyramid is still the 'heaviest' building in the world, with a weight of over five million tonnes! The base, which forms the bottom of an almost regular inclined triangle, is about 227 metres (756 feet) in length, and the vertical height is now 136 metres (454 feet), the original apex having been lost. The highest cathedral nave in Europe – that of Beauvais, in France – would fit almost three times into this vertical height.

The individually shaped stones weigh an average of around 2 tonnes, and some two and a half million of these have been cut and manhandled into place, either by slaves or paid workers using wooden sleds or rollers. The Greek historian Herodotus, writing in the fifth century, when the pyramids were already ancient, said that 100,000 men, working in shifts, were employed for thirty years to raise this single building.

And yet, even while they were accounted the main wonder of the world at a time when the other six still held out against the ravages of time and man, the historians had no idea why these pyramids were built. One Roman architect, Frontinus, compared them to the useful stone aqueducts at Rome, and termed them 'the idle pyramids' – if they had ever had any purpose, then it was no longer known.

It is of course generally believed that the pyramids were vast tombs. Indeed, most of the later small pyramids were in fact mausoleums, and certain of the early large pyramids (such as the Step Pyramid at Saqqarah) were used to bury mummified royal corpses, yet there is no sure evidence that this was their original purpose. It is certain that no pharaoh

The Pyramid group at Giza with the Great Pyramid of Cheops in the far distance. The central large pyramid is that of Chephren, which still retains traces of the original limestone casing towards the top. The smaller pyramid of the three is that of Mycerinus.

was buried in the Great Pyramid, for example. But if there is a shortage of fact about the purpose of these structures, there is no shortage of guesswork and theory, ranging from the ridiculous to the sublime.

It has been suggested that they were gigantic lighthouses for the naval traffic of the Nile; that they were massive ramparts against the invading desert sands; that they were cosmic clocks, regulated to the drift of the stars; and even carefully wrought predictions relating to our own immediate future, warning of the coming of the two World Wars. Careful measurements have revealed many astonishing facts: for example, the ratios within the structure of the Great Pyramid are based on the *pi* ratio of 3·14159, and on the exact number of days in a solar year; not only is the Pyramid orientated precisely to the cardinal points, but it is also located exactly upon the geometric centre and southern extremity of the quadrant which encloses the entire Nile delta! Such facts, allied to the findings of recent researches, would suggest that they had a spiritual purpose – probably to provide initiation chambers and schools for the priestcraft associated with the Egyptian mystery cults relating to the god Osiris and his consort Isis.

An integral part of this complex of pyramids at Giza is the mysterious, crouching Sphinx, which the ancient Egyptians called Hu. It was the Greeks who gave it the name we now use, and sphinx meant in their tongue 'strangler', for they no doubt confused it with their own female-headed, female-breasted monster, who destroyed those unfortunates unable to solve her riddles. The Egyptian Sphinx was no such creature, however, and was supposed to be the material form into which the Egyptian Sun-god Ra would incarnate in order to protect his worshippers. The face is not, as is generally assumed, that of a woman – it is badly eroded, and said by some to be a portrait of the Pharaoh Chephren in his royal headgear and false beard. The figure was carved entire from the living rock, and is about 72 metres (240 feet) long and 20 metres (66 feet) high. To this day people speak of the underground passages which are supposed to be cut into the rocks below, and of the treasure contained in its hidden chambers.

The erosion of the Sphinx reminds us that the ancients would have seen something very different from what meets modern eyes in this remarkable place. Originally there were concourses of temples, mausoleums, ritual chambers and smaller pyramids in ordered profusion around, and there would have been a careful landscaping of trees and plants, where we now see desert sand. There would also have been the Jura limestone which originally covered the outer surface of the pyramids; this was removed by the Arabs only some six centuries ago, and used to build their mosques in Cairo. Such an expanse of white must have been very striking in contrast with the azure Egyptian skies, and perhaps accounts for one of the names given to the Pyramid by the Egyptians: 'the Great Light'. Now of course the unprotected walls are crumbling into decay, and one may only imagine the surface of smooth white light which was known to the ancients.

Of course, the pyramids were very old even for those people we call the ancients. Whilst most modern authorities suggest that the Great Pyramid (by no means the earliest) was constructed around 3350 BC, the age of all pyramids is much disputed. Many argue

Below Cross-section showing the structure of the Great Pyramid, and reconstruction of the site at Giza showing the Pyramids, their temples and approaches. The Great Pyramid is on the left.

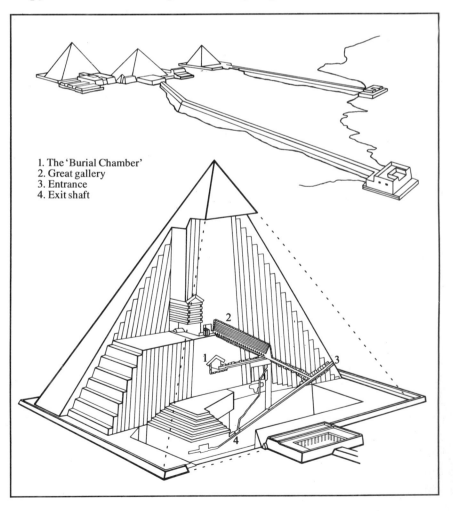

1. The 'Burial Chamber'
2. Great gallery
3. Entrance
4. Exit shaft

that the inscriptions upon which such dating is based were added much later by those who merely restored or modified the buildings. The Sphinx, for example, is of uncertain date, and the inscription between its paws makes it quite clear that even by 1414 BC it was old enough to be completely covered by the desert sands.

One of the most astute of occult historians, the mysterious Madam Blavatsky, suggests that it is reasonable to suppose that the Great Pyramid was built over 80,000 years ago. She bases this claim on the fact that there is a special channel cut through the pyramid which allows the light of the ancient polar star *alpha draconis* to shine down into it. The star's rays would penetrate the pyramid for a few centuries only, gradually inching away with the slow drift of the stars, but returning once in every 78,000 years.

The Greek Herodotus recorded that even in his day the Egyptians had in their possession the statues of 341 god-kings who had reigned over their race, and if one allows only a conservative average of twenty years to each king, then this would put back the historic period of Egyptian culture way beyond anything conceived by modern Egyptologists.

The problem of reconciling such Egyptian records with modern chronology depressed the great Isaac Newton, who found that if he took such lists seriously then the god-kings reigned over Egypt even before the earth was created! Our view of evolution, and our understanding of the age of the earth, has changed since the days of Newton, yet the problem of the antiquity of the pyramids remains much the same. The Italian poet Petrocchi, astounded at the sight of the ancient pyramids, wrote a poem asking Time himself for whom this majestic pile was lifted high, but even Time could not tell, and fled on rapid wings!

The pyramids and the Sphinx are mysteries in stone. In their silent presence one has the feeling that they are somehow eternal, in the true sense of the word, 'outside time' – that they are emerging into visibility from that powerful spiritual world which the ancient Egyptians believed interpenetrated and enriched this material world. Perhaps the secrets of their purpose will remain hidden with the priests, and with that god-king for whom, according to ancient tradition, the plans for the building of the pyramids 'were let down from heaven'.

The Step Pyramid of Zoser at Saqqarah, the earliest surviving large-scale monument built by man.

Karnak

Massive columns in the hypostyle hall of the temple complex of Amon-Ra.

'Amon-Ra, King of the Gods, Creator of the Universe, Lord of Karnak' are some of the names of the supreme god which linked the extraordinary city of Thebes, the capital of ancient Egypt, with the very centre of the spiritual world inhabited by the gods. The Temple at Karnak is the outer form of this god's external glory – no mere place of worship or centre of rituals, as such a temple might be in our own day, but quite seriously regarded as his actual dwelling-place. This vast temple complex has been described as 'a blueprint of the power and glory of a golden era, and a mine of historical information'. Like most important Egyptian temples, it is the work of several pharaohs, each apparently intent on excelling (if not actually obliterating) the work of his predecessor, in manifest devotion to this greatest of all gods.

The result of such a competition among pharaohs is that the temple became a whole religious complex, a city of temples, of temples within temples, courts within courts, chapels, pylons, colonnades and a sacred lake. It is virtually a small walled city dedicated nominally to Amon-Ra, but peppered with chapels and temples to 'guest' deities, and linked by sphinx-lined avenues to the neighbouring temples of Mut, and the vast temple in nearby Luxor (see page 36).

The original Egyptian name for Karnak, which is itself merely a late Arabic name for the town, meant 'the most perfect of places'. The name seems only appropriate for the dwelling of the chief god of Egypt over a period which is, as the archeologist Leonard Cottrell reminds us, longer in duration than the period of Christianity. It is by far the largest temple in the Western world, and to gather from recently revealed secrets recorded by such Egyptologists as Isha Schwaller de Lubicz, one of the most remarkable in design. What it lacks in beauty (that is, in its present depleted form) it certainly makes up in sheer size, to a point where those familiar with it merely stumble over superlatives of length, height, breadth and volume when trying to convey to others the scale of its remaining halls.

The normal procedure is to compare the temple with the better known Christian edifices. Cottrell, for example, makes the point that within the walls of the temple itself (not to mention the precincts!) there is room for St Peter's in Rome, Notre Dame in Paris, and the enormous cathedral of Milan all together. The columns in the hypostyle hall are 10 metres (33 feet) in circumference, with architraves which weigh about 70 tonnes each. Each of these columns will hold a hundred men, standing shoulder to shoulder – provided, of course, that they have no fear of falling the 21-metre (70-foot) drop below their feet! The first great gateway to the temple is over 15 metres (50 feet) thick, which is to say as thick in its wall as many religious buildings are long in their inner space! No wonder that Jean-François Champollion, that great Frenchman who first laboured intelligently and productively with the Egyptian hieroglyphics, should say of the Egyptians, with this particular temple in mind, that they 'thought out their ideas as though they were in fact men a hundred feet tall'.

Even in its partial ruin the place is quite magnificent, its most remarkable hallways and precincts restored without that taint of death which so many restorations bring. Its very size is bewildering for the first-time visitor. The scale of the building and the complexity of its ground-plan are so confusing that any good description of its complex structure must read something like a guided lecture tour. Yet such a tour in the imagination will convey an impression of its size and rich history to anyone intent on visualizing its original grandeur.

The entrance, by way of the first pylon (the word being derived from the Greek, meaning 'gateway', and usually applied to the huge masses of masonry in front of the Egyptian temples) is from the Nile. We approach between a double row of ram-headed sphinxes – the ram being the external form of Amon – with sun-discs on their heads, and a pharaoh between their forepaws. This first pylon is 113 metres (373 feet) wide, and towers above us some 43 metres (142 feet). We are led through

One of the avenues of sphinxes which led originally from the Temple of Amon-Ra to Luxor.

this into the first court, the Great Court, which was built relatively late, during the first millennium BC. Our progress into the temple is in fact a journey by stages backwards in time, if we ignore the time-disturbing restorations and desecrations, which themselves cover a period of somewhat over two thousand years!

Rather surprisingly, in one of the walls of this 9000 sq. metre (97,000 sq. feet) of courtyard, orientated at right-angles to the lengthwise orientation of the temple itself, is a small temple built by Ramses III. This is the only temple still standing in Egypt which was built by a single Pharaoh to a single plan. The court is flanked by sphinxes, and immediately to the left in the yard is a shrine to the famous 'Theban triad' of gods, Amon, Khons (the human-headed Moon-god with seven forms, who may have been the namesake of Chronos, the Greek god of Time) and Mut, the consort of Amon, the world mother.

On the far side of this huge courtyard is the second pylon, in front of which are two huge statues: the one to the left is a red granite figure of Panejem, about 10·5 metres (35 feet) high. When we pass through the second pylon we find ourselves in the Great Hypostyle Hall, which covers an area of 5000 sq. metres (54,000 sq. feet) and which quite takes one's breath away in its size. The guides, who have never been to Paris and do not know who 'Our Lady' is, will tell you that this area will hold the entire cathedral of Notre Dame with great ease. This enormous space is partly hidden by the forest of columns which once supported the roof. There are 134 massive columns, arranged in sixteen rows, in a major feat of engineering begun by Ramses I and completed by Ramses II some generations later. Judging by the great time-scales of Egyptian chronology, this hall was until comparatively recently in considerable ruin: when Napoleon saw it during his ill-fated Egyptian campaign, the columns leaned, and the hall was filled with debris. It was on his orders that it was so effectively restored by French archaeologists. In fact, Napoleon's expedition to Egypt gave considerable impetus to the practice of archaeology.

On the southern wall of this hall is a curious survival – the earliest known text of a non-aggression pact which, like so many pacts, was the result of prolonged aggression. It marks a final agreement between Ramses II and the

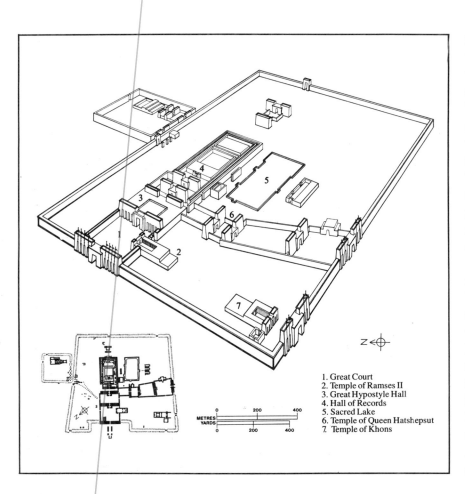

1. Great Court
2. Temple of Ramses II
3. Great Hypostyle Hall
4. Hall of Records
5. Sacred Lake
6. Temple of Queen Hatshepsut
7. Temple of Khons

METRES
YARDS

0   200   400

0   200   400

Three-dimensional plan
of the temple complex.

fresh air of the spiritual world to waft into
the building. The obelisks were so enormous
that when Thutmose III sought to eradicate
all memory of this Queen he hated, even he
baulked at the idea of trying to pull them
down, and he contented himself with having
the monliths blocked in up to the roof in order
that they might not be seen within the temple.
The quarrying of the granite in distant Aswan,
the transportation by boat and roller, and the
installation on a single pedestal, was a
miracle of engineering which was recorded in
one of the reliefs at Dayr al Bahri.

Beyond these colonnades is the fifth pylon,
itself separated from the Sanctuary beyond
by a second colonnade, leading into the
entrance of the sixth pylon, which faces the
vast Hall of Records, built by Thutmose II.
Here were kept the state records relating to
the rich booty and temple gifts received during the years of prosperity which marked this
important Egyptian dynasty. The Sanctuary
beyond is not Egyptian, for the pink granite
chamber was built by Philip, the brother of
Alexander the Great, on the ruins of a much
earlier temple chamber.

Outside the temple, and beyond its complex
of surrounding rooms, we come to a space
which contains the depleted ruins of the
temple of an earlier period (almost 2000 BC),
but our eyes are immediately taken not by the
ruins, so much as by the splendid survival of
the Great Festival Temple of Thutmose III.
This glorious monument is 44 metres (145
feet) wide and 16 metres (53 feet) deep, the
roof being carried by twenty columns in a
double row, with thirty-two square pillars on
the sides. The arrangement is a most curious
one, for Thutmose had the columns designed
so that they tapered inwards towards the
base, which produces a most disturbing
feeling, and an effect which is unique in
Egyptian architecture. The Festival Temple is
surrounded by a complex of small rooms,
including a sanctuary which was restored by
Alexander the Great.

The temple precinct beyond is scattered
with ruins, and includes a sacred lake where
the priests were able to purify themselves in
holy water. This lake is 'guarded' by one of
the enormous scarab beetles placed there by
Amenhotep III.

At right-angles to the main orientation of
the vast Temple of Amon-Ra, leading into
the long avenue of sphinxes directed towards

Hittites, witnessed by thousands of Egyptian
and Hittite deities.

The third pylon, which continues the
temple orientation, takes us through a central
court towards the fourth pylon, built by
Thutmose I, then into a complex colonnade,
towards a fifth pylon constructed by the same
pharaoh. In this colonnade stands the tallest
ancient Egyptian obelisk still standing – a
single block of pink Aswan granite, said to
weigh 328 tonnes, and which towers 29 metres
(97 feet) high, placed there about 1500 BC by
Queen Hatshepsut. This surviving monolith
of the pair erected by the Queen has an inscription which tells how she conceived the
idea of such vast obelisks, 'whose points
might mingle with heaven'. Her remarkable
architect Senmut (who according to legend
was also her lover, and who designed the
wonderful funerary temple of Hatshepsut in
nearby Dayr al Bahri – see page 28) was
commissioned to quarry and erect the stones,
a feat he accomplished in about seven
months. During this time the Queen had the
roof of the hall dismantled, thus neatly
changing the plans of her father, Thutmose I,
in order that the obelisks might be visible
above the temple, allowing, as it were, the

A bas-relief from Karnak (now in the Museum at Cairo), showing the Pharaoh Sesostris I with Ptah, the god of the underworld.

the ruined Temple of Mut, is a series of four pylons enclosing courtyards. The second of these is the oldest part of the temple, and was built by Queen Hatshepsut in around 1500 BC.

To the right of this is the temple dedicated to the Moon-god Khons, which contains one of the rare reliefs showing the Egyptian practice of circumcision (though more ancient examples were discovered at Saqqarah). It suggests that the temple was the scene of circumcision rites for groups of children, who were probably between the ages of four and eight.

This Temple of Khons marks the beginning of the ancient sphinx-lined avenue to Luxor. Such rows of sphinxes, which lined many of the ceremonial routes and important roadways, were originally thought to be merely decorative, but it is more likely that they have a function as guardian forces of the religious precincts and roadways they flank. One ancient inscription upon a sphinx, suggesting that the sphinx was regarded as a kind of amuletic charm on a grand scale, has been recorded and translated: 'I protect the chapel of thy tomb. I guard thy sepulchral chamber. I ward off the intruding stranger. I cast down thy foes to the ground, and their arms with them. I drive away the wicked one from the chapel of thy tomb. I destroy thy adversaries in their lurking places, blocking it that they come forth no more.'

The avenue which led from the Temple of Khons towards Luxor was lined with 122 sandstone sphinxes by Amenhotep III, but these were unlike the Great Sphinx of Giza, which has become the image of the Egyptian classical sphinx. They were in some cases jackal-headed, and ram-headed, rather than with human faces, and they had between their outstretched paws small images of the pharaoh himself. The source for the idea of the sphinx is under much dispute: it has been suggested that it was derived from the huge gate-guardians of Babylon, the winged bulls, but in fact the Great Sphinx is certainly much older than anything found in Babylon, and it might well be that the idea of a stone 'protective guardian' was adopted by the Babylonians from the Egyptians. The presence of sphinxes, in different forms, in early Mediterranean civilizations most probably points to the immense influence of the highly developed civilization of the Egyptians, of which this city of Karnak was a crowning glory.

The Temple of Queen Hatshepsut

The mortuary temple of Queen Hatshepsut, inset into the rocks of the Theban hills at Dayr al Bahri in a unique system of terraces and colonnades, has been described by the historian, Leonard Cottrell, as being 'in some ways the most impressive work of man in Egypt'.

It was built by the queen's architect Senmut – one of the earliest artists to emerge with a personality and character of his own – in the fifteenth century before Christ, but contrary to popular notions it was never intended to house the body of the queen herself, and nor is it strictly speaking a temple. It might more accurately be described as a religious precinct, for within its gracious colonnades and terraces there are a large number of temples and shrines. These include several dedicated to Amon, the most important of all the gods in Luxor, whose name is almost certainly related to the modern Christian invocation Amen, which meant in Egyptian 'that which is concealed'. Other temples were dedicated to Anubis, Hathor and Ra. Anubis, a jackal-headed deity who was linked with the Egyptian death cults and mummification, was an important figure in the rites carried out over a dead person. The goddess Hathor was often portrayed with the horns or ears of a cow, and ruled over love, beauty, happiness and music; it was believed that seven Hathors would come to a new-born child to decide on what kind of life he was to have. The temple to Hathor is the best preserved one in the terraces. Finally, Ra was the sun-god and held in some traditions to have created mankind, and accordingly the Egyptians called themselves 'the cattle of Ra'. Open-air sacrifices were held at his temple each day at dawn.

The body of Queen Hatshepsut herself was buried in a rock tomb in the western side of the cliffs, some distance from the religious precinct built on her behalf, which was intended mainly as a site for post-mortem religious observations. The fact that when the temple was finished an avenue of sphinxes was constructed leading from it to the valley would suggest that the burial was not merely a matter of secrecy, intended to foil tomb-robbers.

An aerial view of the funerary temple of Queen Hatshepsut at Dayr al Bahri, near ancient Thebes (Luxor).

The temple is excellently sited against the backdrop of the Theban hills, and gives the impression of being an organic element of them, a natural outgrowth of rare beauty rather than something man-made added on. There are three main levels of terraces, around which the mortuary chapels are constructed, the approach being by way of the central monumental ramp and stairways.

The middle terrace has to the right the well-preserved Hathor sanctuary, and to the left the sanctuary of Anubis (which contains the famous 'Punt' reliefs, which we shall examine shortly).

Bas-relief from the Hathor sanctuary in the mortuary temple of Queen Hatshepsut. The goddess Hathor is shown in the incarnate form of a cow, licking the hand of the Queen.

The upper terrace is a walled court lined with a double colonnade, to the left of which is the mortuary chapel of Queen Hatshepsut, and to the right the chapel dedicated to Ra. The main sanctuary lies behind the upper court, and is cut into the solid rock of the hillside.

In the Anubis temple or chapel there are two sets of reliefs, both of which reflect upon the essentially peaceful nature of the reign of Hatshepsut. One set shows the transportation of two enormous obelisks designed for the temple of Amon in Karnak, one of which still stands inside the temple, some 30 metres (97 feet) high, weighing 328 tonnes.

The other set of reliefs is an account of the visit to the land of Punt, to 'God's Land', as the ancient Egyptians termed the place which is now generally accepted by historians as being Somaliland in East Africa. This expedition, made famous in history almost entirely by these reliefs, took place in the ninth year of Queen Hatshepsut's reign, which is to say at about the same time as work on her mortuary temple was begun.

The presence of these reliefs in Dayr al Bahri has given rise to many interesting speculations, for within them we see images of five ocean-going vessels, berthing in Thebes itself. Now since Thebes is by no means a natural harbour (the Nile which flows through the modern Karnak would never float a large ship), this has naturally led people to suggest that there might at one time have been a vast canal system between the Nile and the Red Sea (an idea which actually has some support in ancient literature). There is no physical trace of such a canal, however, and therefore many modern historians are inclined to regard the reliefs as being based on imagination. Perhaps if these reliefs had not been placed alongside the others which tell the story of the transportation of the obelisks, a known historical event, then it would have been easier to dismiss the factuality of these 'Theban docks'.

It was in Dayr al Bahri, also, that Emil Brugsch made a miraculous find of the accumulated mummies of the pharaohs which had lain relatively untouched for millennia. He discovered the cache by acting on information given against robbers who had located the tomb, and who were already involved in removing its riches when he arrived. Within this mass burial ground he found the mummies of nearly fifty kings, queens and high officials, including Ramses II and III, and Queen Nefertari. Among the mummies was that of Thutmose III, who was the ignoble half-brother and son-in-law of Queen Hatshepsut. In an attempt to efface the memory of her reign Thutmose so damaged the mortuary temple of Hatshepsut as to necessitate modern restorations.

Left The Egyptian gods Ra (*left*), Anubis (*centre*) and Hathor, all of whom have temples within the precinct.
Below An aerial view of the funerary temple at Dayr al Bahri, taken from above the range of cliffs to show the inside of the temple complex.

The Tomb of Tutankhamen

'Surely never before in the whole history of excavation had such an amazing sight been seen as the light of our torches revealed to us', exclaimed the archaeologist, Howard Carter, describing his experience after breaking the ancient seals, and passing through the doorway leading into the underground burial chamber of Tutankhamen in 1922. Carter had worked painstakingly and methodically for years in the lunar landscape Valley of the Kings to the west of Luxor, in order to discover the very thing which now lay before him. Even he had not yet realized at that point just how valuable the contents of this ancient tomb would prove to be.

Within the complex of the tomb, Carter and his assistants found the mummified body of the ancient boy-king Tutankhamen, who had ruled supreme in Egypt for a few short years round about 1350 BC. As is rare in such Egyptian finds, the mummified body was quite untouched by grave-robbers, and it was for the very first time that archaeologists were able to form a directly personal impression of the burial state of a pharaoh.

The body was bedecked with gold and precious stones, and over the mummy itself was the now famous portrait mask of gold, inland with lapis lazuli, turquoise, cornelian, obsidian and faience, bearing over its forehead the insignia of royalty, the vulture and cobra, in solid gold.

The coffin in which this richly swathed body was placed was itself covered in gold, but this was fitted within a second coffin, 1·8 metres (6 feet) long, which proved to be made of solid gold, weighing some 110 kilos (242 lb), and enormously valuable. This was in turn placed within a third gold-covered coffin, encrusted with semi-precious stones, and the whole nest of coffins was contained in a quartzite sarcophagus, about 1·5 metres (5 feet) square in cross-section, and about 2·7 metres (9 feet) long. The lid, which weighed 610 kilos (12 cwt) was carved from rose-coloured granite. This entire series of coffins and sarcophagus was enclosed in a magnificent burial shrine, which measured 2·7 metres (9 feet) high and 5·1 by 3·3 metres (17 by 11 feet), covered completely in gold. Nothing like this had ever been found by an archaeologist before.

Around the shrine, and in adjacent chambers, was found a most amazing collection of personal and public property which had been used by the king during his lifetime. There were chairs, tables and couches, all of exquisite workmanship and design; four beautiful chariots faced in gold (with wheelbases so wide that the axles had had to be cut in two in order to get them into the tomb); there were ritual objects, images of the pharaoh in gold, breath-takingly beautiful pectorals, necklaces of gold and precious stones, knives of refined craftsmanship, miniature effigies, seals and rings – and it was all beyond price.

Perhaps the most moving experience for Carter was that magical moment when he slowly removed the portrait mask, and then the swathing of the bandages, to look upon the face of this long-dead pharaoh, which was, in Carter's words, 'refined and cultured, the features well-formed, especially the clearly marked lips'. Actually, the photographs show the visage twisted in the terrible grimace of death, but one may imagine the wonder with which Carter gazed down upon the face, perhaps for him the richest prize within the tomb.

That such riches in gold and precious stones should be deposited in a tomb may well surprise us nowadays, for we have a view of death which is very different from that of the ancient Egyptians. The dividing line between life and death was obviously not so clearly defined for them as it is for us: the life of spirit which surrounded men in the living world was believed to continue in that other world, with the difference that what was under normal circumstances invisible to

The gold and inlaid mask which covered the mummified body of the young Pharaoh Tutankhamen.

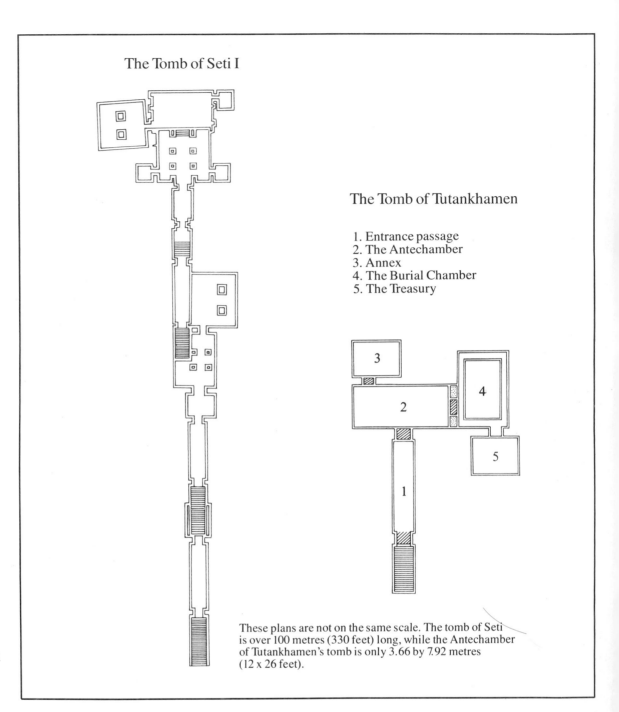

The Tomb of Seti I

The Tomb of Tutankhamen

1. Entrance passage
2. The Antechamber
3. Annex
4. The Burial Chamber
5. The Treasury

These plans are not on the same scale. The tomb of Seti is over 100 metres (330 feet) long, while the Antechamber of Tutankhamen's tomb is only 3.66 by 7.92 metres (12 x 26 feet).

Plans of the tombs of Tutankhamen (right) and Seti I showing the difference in their complexity.

ordinary eyesight during life became quite visible after death. The Egyptian god Thoth, who was the early form of the Roman Mercury, was said to preside over the moment of death. He was described as 'the god who opens the eyes at death' – in other words, the human soul only begins to see properly on dying, and during lifetime it lives partly in an illusion. Life after death was not merely an absolute certainty for the Egyptian priests, and for the people they served, but it is likely that even the rules governing non-physical life were clearly laid down. This knowledge enabled them to construct magic rites and rituals in order to guide the newly dead per-son through the realms which he or she would first encounter after a lifetime in the physical body. It is this concept of the 'reality' of the post-mortem states which accounts for much of the complex ceremonial involved in burying important individuals.

The large number of passwords and rituals which are found in the Egyptian Book of the Dead (a collection of scripts relating to the post-mortem life) are keys to the various stages in the pathways though some of the tombs. Thus the space of such tombs reflects the structure of this literary collection of spells and invocations. In fact, the tomb of Tutankhamen is an exception to this general rule, for it was apparently not built to house the body of the boy-king, who died before his huge mausoleum was finished. Because of this, the few chambers within this tomb complex do not express a relationship with the Book of the Dead texts.

Surprisingly little is known about the Pharaoh Tutankhamen. His name means either 'the living image of Aten', or 'the Life of Amon is pleasing'. His parentage is unclear, but he was probably related to the 'heretic' Pharaoh Akhenaton. He came to the throne of Egypt when he was only nine years old, and ruled for about the same number of years, spending much of his time in Memphis and Thebes, which was at that time the capital of Egypt. He proved to be the last of his dynasty, and the two miniature coffins with stillborn children placed near his own sarcophagus might have been the product of his union with his wife Ankhesenamen.

The fact is that Tutankhamen ruled over a vast and wealthy nation at the height of its glory and culture, yet he was by no means the most important or significant of Egyptian rulers. Bearing this in mind, and thinking of the riches within his burial chamber, we might imagine the splendour which must have attended the burial of such a pharaoh as Ramses II, whose magnificent, not to say megalomanic, life on earth was on a level far removed from that of the boy-king.

None of the many important tombs in the necropolis of this Valley of the Kings has ever yielded such treasures as these (the theft of buried treasures from such tombs had been a speciality of certain Egyptian families for many generations, and has only to some small extent been curtailed by modern archaeology), yet the very size and complexity of many of the surrounding tombs hint at further secrets yet to be revealed. Some of these neighbouring tombs make a most interesting comparison with the relatively modest chambers of Tutankhamen. For example, the complex tomb of Seti I, which was discovered in 1817 by the circus strongman Belzoni, who became an archaeologist almost by accident, is a system of passageways and chambers which does relate to the various stages set out in the Egyptian Book of the Dead. The tomb is over 100 metres (330 feet) in length, with steps leading deeper and deeper into the bowels of the rock, ter-

minating in a huge burial chamber which is lavishly decorated and especially famous for the astrological frescoes on the ceiling and walls (although these have, in fact, almost nothing to do with modern astrology).

This tomb may well contain a secret which will remain hidden from modern eyes. The Egyptian Department of Antiquities only a few years ago received information of an oral tradition that beyond the burial chamber itself there was (quite contrary to normal Egyptian burial practices) a further chamber, connected to it by a long passageway. After only a fairly simple survey, such a passage was indeed discovered: it continued the general downward direction of the passages into the earth, and since it had been filled with rubble, as was often the practice in Egyptian burials, work was started to dig it out. However, after some 90 metres (300 feet) had been cleared, the work was discontinued as it was proving both dangerous to the tomb of Seti itself, and too exhausting for the workers. Perhaps one day a method may be devised for a thorough examination of this passageway, and its terminal chambers and their contents, hidden for thousands of years – even from the tomb-robbers – may be revealed. It is of course not to be expected that anything of the order of Tutankhamen's tomb will be discovered in the future in this desolate Valley of the Kings, but it is likely that not all its secrets have yet been disclosed to the world of the living.

An example of the rich burial treasure found in the tomb of Tutankhamen.

Luxor

When the invading Arabs came to the south of Egypt and saw the temples of ancient Thebes, they called them 'castles', *el Uqsor*, which became 'Luxor' in the mouths of Europeans. One of these Arabic 'castles' is the Temple of Luxor, which is usually ascribed to the Pharaoh Amenhotep III. He built much of it around 1400 BC, although like most Egyptian temples many pharaohs and non-pharaohs lent their hands both to it and against it. The temple which now remains was officially built between 1408 and 1300 BC, but it has been knocked about by several nations and by many religious groups since then, and one or two important constructions and frescoes are of a much later date. A short walk along the length of the temple, which is designed (along established Egyptian lines) as a stage by stage processional to the inner sanctum where the god was supposed to dwell, may reveal a little of its complex history.

The visitor must enter by way of the 'gateway' or pylon, which leads into the first courtyard. This is the first of a series of huge pylons and it was an afterthought, erected by Ramses II. He also built some obelisks and six colossal statues of himself in a typical large-scale piece of advertising which still works its subliminal magic since visitors, suitably dwarfed by his figures, tend to think that Ramses constructed the entire building. One of the pink granite obelisks in front of the first pylon has hieroglyphics upon the base which actually proclaim the lie that Ramses built the temple. The reliefs carved on the wall of the pylon also boast of Ramses, for they tell the somewhat vainglorious story of his military conquests against the Hittites, who are shown in great fear before this superhuman pharaoh.

Something of the curious history of the temple begins to dawn on the visitor when he passes through the pylon into the first courtyard, for to the left, built into the walls and colonnades, is the incongruous mosque of

The first pylon, or gateway, of the Temple of Luxor, fronted by two colossal statues of Ramses II.

Abu el Hagag, not only still used to this day, but actually quite recently extended! The court and mosque are set in a surround of beautiful papyrus columns with lotus-head capitals, where we find more statues of the ubiquitous Ramses.

Once out of this courtyard we enter the realm proper of Amenhotep. The famous boy-king Tutankhamen had the walls decorated with reliefs depicting the Great New Year festival. This was dedicated to the god Opet, and the flooded Nile became the scene of merry-making for twenty-four days, with sacrifices to the gods, displays of dancing girls, sideshows, rituals, and all the many human delights which might honour the god Amon, who was at the time supposed to be visiting the harem.

Beyond the colonnade is the Court of Amenhotep which contains three seated statues, two of the gods Amon and Mut, and the third of Ramses II. This courtyard leads into a hypostyle (a colonnaded entrance-way) of enormous columns, arranged in four groups of eight, with a few remaining reliefs which show Amenhotep involved in religious rituals. Here we find a curious amendment to the Egyptian plan, for there is a very Roman altar dedicated to the Emperor Augustus. Some of the columns in this part of the temple were removed when the Christians continued the work of the supporters of Augustus, adopting the temple for their own religion some two thousand years after it had been dedicated to Amon. (This later use has its ironies, as the word 'amen' is almost certainly a derivation from the name of this Egyptian god.)

The next group of buildings are chambers which originally surrounded the sanctuary of the gods. The Christian modifications have damaged these, but we may still examine the important murals in the 'birth room' which are once again a subtle piece of advertising – this time on behalf of Amenhotep. These pictures attempt to clear up some of the (quite reasonable) doubts regarding his legitimacy to rule as pharaoh. They are designed to leave one in no doubt that he was of the required royal birth, for we see no less a god than Amon embracing his mother, and hence fertilizing her, with the sequel of her pregnancy and delivery of the child of this celestial union, who was to be Pharaoh Amenhotep himself.

In the midst of these surrounding rooms was the original Egyptian 'Holy of Holies', a sanctuary where a golden statue of the god Amon was daily cleansed, clothed and perfumed by the many priestesses. The name of the sanctuary has disappeared along with the statue, for it is now called the Sanctuary of Alexander the Great, as this Greek genius rebuilt the entire area and installed his own shrine in place of that of Amon. Much later the area was adapted to an even more sacrilegious purpose. It became the living room of the French engineer delegated to supervise the removal of the great pink granite obelisk which had balanced the one still standing at the entrance to the temple, in order that it might be re-sited in the Place de la Concorde, in Paris.

Ancient Thebes, as capital of Egypt, was a centre renowned for more than its huge temples, of course. At the height of Egyptian civilization, during what we now call the New Kingdom, the city must have been vast. The Temple of Luxor stands on the east bank of the Nile, and around it have gathered the main hotels in modern times to cater for tourists. Further to the north is a magnificent and altogether too colossal Temple to Amon-Ra (see page 24), which was at one time joined to modern Luxor by a sphinx-lined processional avenue. No doubt these two, and the smaller Temple of Mut which stood between them, also linked by sphinx-lined avenues, were surrounded by palaces and private homes as well as by innumerable small houses; the city probably stretched along the banks of the Nile for some considerable distance.

On the other side of the river are the remains of many other temples, further indications of the size of the place. Starting at the north, and moving south-west, we find the Temple of Seti I, that of Thutmose III, and then the Temple of Amenhotep, along with that dedicated to Thoth, rounded off by the remains of the Palace of Enophis III. Between the Temples of Thutmose and Amenhotep stands the huge and sadly ruined Ramesseum, silent testimony to the megalomania of this pharaoh (which we may see in a kinder form at Abu Simbel – see page 40), with a fallen and broken statue of himself estimated to weigh over 1000 tonnes.

Near this, though isolated and lonely in the flat fields, are the most famous of all Egyptian statues after the Sphinx: the statues of Memnon, one of which was said to greet the dawn with a song. These colossi were dubbed by the Romans with the title of one of their mythical heroes because of this connection with the rising sun (Memnon was the son of Aurora, the Roman goddess of the dawn). A few of the many Greek and Latin inscriptions cut into the limestone statues confirm that the 'singing' had been heard. Modern explanations for the sound, which was said to vary from a sweet musical harmony to angry chanting, is that the different blocks from which the statues are made expanded at different rates in the warmth of the morning sun, scraping together and so producing the noise. This explanation is conjectural, however, for the statues sing no more. The Roman Emperor Septimius Severus had the colossi repaired, and from that moment they have remained silent. The curious weathering of these statues has contributed to the strangeness of their appearance, as does their apparent isolation on this flat area of fertile ground. Originally they formed the entrance to a mortuary temple of Amenhotep III, but behind them now is a wasteland of poor grass, grazed by goats.

Behind and beyond this fairly desolate area of the once-thriving Thebes is the backcloth of steep hills and cliffs which were used for burials and funerary temples. To the south is the famous Valley of the Queens, to the north the even more famous Valley of the Kings, well known in modern times for its rich yield of treasures from the tomb of the boy-king Tutankhamen (see page 32). In the cliff face itself, to the west (so that from its colonnaded terrace, one might see across the Nile to the Temples of Luxor and Karnak) is the funerary monument of Queen Hatshepsut (see page 28). Behind this, hidden in the rocks, was the secret burial place of the collected mummies of the ancient royalty and retinue of Egypt, which are now lodged safely away from the grave-robbers in the Museum at Cairo. The various temples and centres named above are all part of the original Thebes, and all fall into an area of approximately 65 sq. km (25 sq. miles), yet this is presumed to be merely the vestigial remains of what must at one time have been a vast metropolis and temple complex, sprawling over an enormous area along the banks of the Nile.

The Temple of Luxor, viewed from across the Nile.

Abu Simbel

The temples at Abu Simbel in Upper Egypt might well have been listed as one of the Great Wonders of the ancient world, for in a sense they are the reverse of the pyramids. Standing before the pyramids we find it hard to believe that such masses of masonry could have been constructed by man; standing in the dark confines of the temples of Abu Simbel, we find it quite incredible that so much interior space could have been sculpted from a single massive cliff of solid sandstone. The temples of Abu Simbel are described as though they were buildings – in terms quite appropriate to architecture – but it is in fact more accurate to consider them as enormous sculptures.

The two main temples are located on the western bank of the Nile, about 270 kilometres (168 miles) south of Aswan, and were built by Ramses II between 1300 and 1233 BC.

The larger temple is dedicated to Ptah, the god of the underworld, Amon, and to Harakhte, a form of the sun god Horus. The solid front of this temple consists of four seated figures of the pharaoh, Ramses II, cut into the living rock, each over 20 metres (65 feet) high, within a temple façade 36 metres (119 feet) long and 32 metres (105 feet) high. There are smaller (though larger than life-size) figures of the royal family set between them, for example, the mother of Ramses, Queen Ti, and Queen Nefertari, his favourite wife. This group of statuary is impressive enough, but the imposing doorway leads inside the sculpture, within the solid rock, into the first of the three main halls which measures 16·2 metres (54 feet) across and 17·4 metres (58 feet) deep. To see the temple stretching out far beyond, into the darkness of this man-made space, can induce a vertigo similar to that often experienced by first-time visitors to the pyramids. This great hypostyle has eight columns cut from the rock, faced with huge statues of Ramses II in the guise of the god Osiris, and is painted throughout.

The second hall is supported by four pillars, and is 10·8 by 7·5 metres (36 by 25 feet), with wall reliefs showing Ramses and his wife Nefertari burning incense, and the pharaoh with his chariot. The third hallway is the sanctuary itself, with four seated figures – the three gods to whom the temple was dedicated, with the inevitable figure of Ramses alongside them.

The nearby Temple of Nefertari, which is actually a temple dedicated to Hathor, also built by Ramses II, is sometimes called the 'small temple' yet it has a frontage of six huge statues, 10 metres (33 feet) high, within an area on the cliff face some 27 metres (90 feet) long by 12 metres (40 feet) high. This temple is virtually a family portrait in sandstone, for four of the statues are of Ramses himself, two are of his wife, whilst the smaller figures around them are those of their children. Within, the hypostyle hall is supported by six pillars with the characteristic archaic heads of the goddess Hathor, and inside the sanctuary at the back there are impressive reliefs of Nefertari and the goddess. It was this same Nefertari, deified here as wife of the god-king Ramses, who was one of the mummified remains found in the secret burial chamber at Dayr al Bahri, and which are now in Cairo Museum.

These temples were used until well into the Christian era, but were eventually covered over by the natural drift of the sands, until they were finally forgotten. The Swiss explorer Burckhardt found them in 1813, and they naturally became the focus of much archaeological activity. When it was realized that the projected damming of the Nile to form the Aswan dam would leave the temples inundated, a vast engineering scheme was adopted by which these temples, along with another thirty huge monuments and temples, were lifted higher up the cliff face. A wall was constructed around the temple to protect it from the rising waters of the Nile,

Bas-relief from the Great Temple at Abu Simbel.

Below View of the two rock temples at Abu Simbel, both built by the Pharaoh Ramses II. The one to the left (with the four colossal figures of Ramses) is the Great Temple, and the one to the right is the smaller Temple of Nefertari, which was dedicated to Hathor.

and then it was cut up into manageable cubes (some 400,000 tonnes of sandstone being handled in this way), which were lifted out and reassembled on top of the cliff, nearly 30 metres (100 feet) above the old site.

It was one of the great salvage feats of modern times, but inevitably, something was lost. Before the temples were re-sited, there was a time of year when the rays of the rising sun would strike through the doorway of the main temple, to penetrate its full 54-metre (180-foot) length, and fall for a few moments on the rear wall where the statues of the gods and the pharaoh were seated. Travellers who experienced this wonder of lighting would speak of it in reverential terms, for it was one of the earliest known uses of direct sunlight for conveying a meaning within a temple – a method adopted by the later Christian builders in Europe. Now, of course, with the temple façades and innards having been lifted bodily from their original position, it has been impossible to duplicate this light effect.

THE
MIDDLE
EAST

View of rock-hewn tombs in the desert city of
Petra, in modern Jordan.

Ur

Anyone interested in ancient history who has travelled across the desert areas of Iraq by land and also by air, will know how different are the two experiences. Driving across the desert, you see occasional mounds of dust and rubble which only prior knowledge can identify to be the remains of ancient civilizations. If you fly over the same area, you will be able to see the traces of canal systems and road networks that connect the larger piles of dust, which themselves now take on a new perspective of walls, squares and precincts, as if on some faded architectural plan. It is as though you have the vision of one of the gods whom that civilization was built to serve, and are so privileged as to be permitted to see into the wonders of the vanished past.

The Sumerians who occupied these areas some four millennia ago possessed an elaborate system of laws, a wide and well-developed artistic culture, a highly trained and efficient army, and, along with an extensive pantheon of gods, a religious system which was totally integrated into the daily life of the people. It was in the land of Ur, as Sumer has been called, that many of the things we take for granted in our own world were forged, for it was here, as Andrae, one of the archaeologists who worked in the area, remarked, that the 'gods bequeathed the earth to mankind'. The gods gave man the earth and civilization, and in return man built temples and precincts to serve these gods, and worshipped them faithfully and fearlessly in both peace and war. It is this powerful religious feeling which lent a coherence to the civilization of the ancient worlds, and which lies at the roots of our own culture.

The strength of the link between the gods and man is perhaps not well understood in modern times, and in order to grasp fully the living reality of these ancient religions we will have to relax many of our prejudices. In this connection, for example, while it may have at best merely a symbolic significance, we may note that one of the surviving temple-shrines in Uruk has a top step intended to lead into the upper temple. This step is a metre (over 3 feet) high, and is obviously not designed for a human being to mount: it was intended for a divinity to set down into the world from the higher heavens!

The only significant standing monument from this ancient Sumerian past is the huge ziggurat, or stepped temple, in Ur. It appears originally to have been a mass of solid brickwork 63 by 42 metres (210 by 140 feet), in the form of an accentuated series of steps, rising in four main plateaus to a height of 16 metres (54 feet), at the top of which was a sacred shrine. The ziggurat was approached by a triple series of stairs, two contiguous with the masonry, and one facing directly on to it. These flights of steps are restored and well-preserved and are extremely impressive.

The ziggurat stood in the western corner of a sacred precinct which appears to have been dedicated to the Moon-god Nanna, who was the patron god of Ur. The triple staircase connects it to a temple dedicated to Nanna and his consort Ningal, which is in turn connected to a huge courtyard, flanked on all sides with temple buildings. To the southeast, yet still within the temple precinct, were more temples, dedicated to a variety of gods. There are also still some remains of what

Aerial view of the ziggurat and the temple precinct remains at Ur.

intermittent attempts to reconstruct the area, it was not until the reign of Nebuchadnezzar that the ziggurat was restored, and the great convent to the south-east was built, within the precinct. This resoration was short-lived, however, for Cyrus the Great eventually cut through the area, and though he did not destroy it, the Zoroastrian religion was soon imposed to replace the worship of the Moon-god, so that from the third century BC, the site fell into further ruin.

Excavations in the land of Ur have shown that many of the Sumerian kings named on the incredible lists preserved by the Babylonian priest Berossus, and handed on to the Greeks for safe-keeping, were not merely fictitious and legendary. Many of the earlier kings were said to be gods, and those who reigned 'before the Flood' were quite definitely regarded as divine. The last of these was Utnapishtim, who plays a part in the drama of the ancient epic of Gilgamesh, as he was the god-king who achieved immortality, the secret which Gilgamesh himself wished to learn. Towards this end Gilgamesh sacrificed everything, including his love, and his closest friend, Enkidu, in the course of a journey to the ends of the world to seek out Utnapishtim. Yet, for all this sacrifice he did not manage to learn the secret of immortality, which was forbidden even to demi-gods, for the secret had been stolen by a snake; he learned instead the wonderful secret of being a complete human being. This epic, though badly mutilated, and often translated without any real feeling for the inner content of the story itself, is one of the most illuminating

used to be huge walls, built by Nebuchadnezzar, which surrounded this precinct. These separated the temple area from the town itself, which consisted mainly of two-storey brick houses with central courtyards, often containing private chapels, beneath which were the communal burial vaults for the family.

The original city and precinct were apparently laid waste round about 1800 BC, when the inhabitants rebelled against the Babylonian overlords, and, although there were

Reconstruction of the ziggurat.

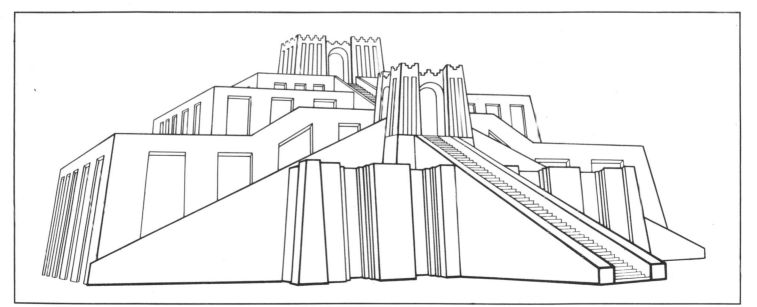

Above Assyrian high relief (from Khorsabad) showing the great King Gilgamesh. The lion cub and the curiously shaped knife are symbols of regal power.

Right Detail of the gold and inlaid figure of the Assyrian ram standing guard by a stylized tree now in the British Museum, London.

documents to come down from those times.

Gilgamesh, for all his remoteness within his god-like sheath, and for all that he walked on the same level as the winged gods, and was said to be two-thirds god himself, was almost modern in his inner disposition. He rebelled against the lot which the gods bequeathed to men, yearning for the ancient sense of eternity which the direct contact with the spiritual world allowed and fostered. But, as one of the later clay tablets laments, 'the gods had withdrawn from the land', and the rebellion of Gilgamesh could lead nowhere, but back to the world, to a closer and more loving relationship with the earth itself. Thus the epic ends with Gilgamesh, a wiser person for his rebellion, being allowed to visit his dead friend Enkidu in that shadowy hell or purgatory in the very centre of the earth.

This Gilgamesh was indeed a real king, and had dwelt in the city of Uruk, in the land of Ur, ruling over the entire area. In Sumerian legend it was Gilgamesh who built the walls around Uruk, and clay tablets have been found witnessing this immense labour. The walls, excavated in 1934, were originally about 6 metres (20 feet) high, about 4·5 metres (15 feet) thick, and 13 kilometres (8 miles) long.

The rich yields of treasure which archaeologists brought to light in the so-called 'death pits' of Ur and related settlements are quite remarkable, and now are among the richest exhibits in the Museum at Baghdad. Perhaps more impressive than the fine works of art which emerge from these pits is the story of the sacrifice of the servants and retinue of those important personages buried there. The archaeologist Sir Leonard Woolley leaves a touching record: 'the floor of the death-pit was covered with bodies all in ordered rows: 6 men on the entrance side, and 68 women in court dress, red coats with beaded cuffs and shell-ring belts, head-dresses of gold or silver, great lunate earrings and multiple necklaces of blue and gold. Among them was one girl who was not wearing her silver hair-ribbon – it was in her pocket, tightly coiled up, as if she had been late for the funeral (her own!) and had not had time to put it on. There were four harpists with their lyres, and by them, in an open space, lay a copper cauldron: it was difficult not to connect this with the little drinking-vessel found by every one of the 74 bodies in the pit.'

Petra

About the only thing we know for sure about Petra is that it is the site of a pre-Christian Nabataean city designed to serve the Arabian caravan routes. We also know that the biblical scholar John Burgon said it was 'a rose-red city, half as old as time'. However, Burgon failed to notice that Petra is not rose-red at all, but an even more exciting spectrum of oranges, vermilions, yellows and purples, set off in delicate blues and greens. It is ironic that such a remarkable man as Burgon (who was in infancy dedicated to the goddess Athena in the Parthenon on the Acropolis), described in his official biography as 'a leading champion of lost causes and impossible beliefs', should now be chiefly remembered for something he got wrong about Petra. When Edward Lear, another distinguished Victorian (better known for his limericks than for his fine topographical drawings) visited the city with his cook Giorgio, the Italian looked around him and said, 'O master, we have come into a world where everything is made of chocolate, ham, curry-powder and salmon' – natural imagery which gives a finer impression of this place than Burgon's famous quote.

Petra is not only multi-coloured rather than rose-red, it is not even a city. Almost all the important remains in this curious, secluded place are tombs, which makes Petra a necropolis, a vast burial ground with even the bodies removed. The cliffs which encircle it are honeycombed with tombs, most of them of a very simple nature, scarcely more than dark doorways let into the stone, but some of them are ornate and wonderful, much like Christian churches misplaced in time and space. One might even construct a convincing thesis to prove that the great Italian artists Bernini and Borromini were brought here as children, and then carried these designs to Rome in the seventeenth century, and in this way passed on Petra to Europe.

Julian Huxley, who visited Petra briefly some years ago, left a description of the natural beauties of the area. He included a poetic account of following the narrow torrent bed which leads to the necropolis, in which one may still see the remains of stone-block pavements, and from which one can only catch glimpses of the sunlight far above, at the top of the towering cliff-face. He turned the bend, and saw a vision of pilasters and architraves: 'instead of shadows, sunlight – instead of nature, art'.

Directly opposite this opening of the *siq*, as the defile is called, is one of the most pleasing of Nabataean monuments, the so-called Treasury of Pharaoh, which has nothing to do with any Egyptian Pharaoh, and which is certainly not a treasury, for the inside of the three chambers was intended to house the body of one of the later Nabataean kings. Built about the beginning of our own era, in the style which we would now recognize as a temple façade of the classical period, it is not so much a building as sculpture carved out of the living rock. The huge solid urn which forms part of the Treasury has been badly chipped, indicating how the evocative misnomers 'Treasury' and 'Pharaoh' arouse greed in the minds of men.

Like all ruins, Petra has been enriched by legends of treasures, unguarded but hidden, and the legends have persisted, even though no treasure has been found in historic times. The richness of Petra lies in its beauty, in its atmosphere, in the fact that it has all the qualities of the archetypal ruin which, as the travel writer Aubrey Menen puts it so well, 'all of us secretly hoped would be discovered on the far side of the Moon'.

Like the far side of the moon, Petra has been photographed, and even visited, but almost nothing is known about its origin or its nature. Even the idea that it was built to serve the caravan routes is little more than an educated guess. But its very seclusion in the

Part of the amphitheatre carved from the rock in Petra.

narrow defile of the dried-up river must have
been welcome to the weary travellers who for
days had been surrounded by that threaten-
ing space which only those used to desert
travel can tolerate for long. Within the defile
there would have been luxurious vegetation
(for the ancient Petra had cisterns designed to
collect the ducted water), teeming humanity
speaking various languages, and the necessary forms of rest and amusement most wel-

come to the lonely traveller. But by the
standards of the day, Petra would have by
no means been an exceptional place, and it
is exceptional today only because it has
survived, and because much of what has
survived is hollowed out from the cliff faces.

When the Romans took over the area, as
was the way of the Romans, they left their
special signature in the form of the theatre
which, like the rock-tombs, is carved from

Above Façade of the rock
tomb of Rabel II, the last
Nabataean King.

the rock. The upper back areas of these ranges of seats have been carved into yet more tombs, encouraging one wit to insist that these were intended to enable the dead to watch the performance below.

Such Roman remains were built after AD 106, when this area was brought into the protective custody of the Empire, but little is now left standing, save for a few stones of a temple, and a triple triumphal arch. Archaeological surveys have revealed that the centre was a huge one – with three market areas, as would befit its position on a caravan route – a forum and portico, with a number of colonnades. No traces have been found in the midst of this Romanization of the free-standing buildings of the Nabataeans.

We can only imagine the drama of this bustling travel centre, with the loaded camels arriving from Arabia, or leaving for Damascus, carrying specialist commodities for the luxury markets of the West and East, and bearing with them also the ideas which would make the history of our age.

Right The so-called Treasury of Pharaoh, which is actually a tomb sculpted out of the rock.

Persepolis

The ancient Persian Empire lasted for only two centuries – not long in the lifetimes of nations. It was born with Cyrus the Great, and met its death at the hands of Alexander the Great, in the fourth century BC. Yet during these two centuries Persia attained an astonishingly high level of civilization. Cyrus the Great was 'great' on a scale which almost defies imagination. He founded an Empire which was to become the largest in the world, with sufficient manpower and resources to throw an army of two million soldiers, not including slaves and camp-followers, against the Greeks, and, in order to make such an invasion possible, to bridge the Hellespont with boats, and to cut across the slopes of Mount Athos with a canal!

There were three capitals to this vast Empire: Susa, which was the political and administrative centre; Pasargadae, the ritual-religious centre used, for example, for the coronation of the kings; and Persepolis, which was a ceremonial centre, and which served as a burial place for members of the dynasty. Cyrus himself was buried at Pasargadae, but Darius and his successors were buried in rock tombs at Naqsh-e-Rostam, near Persepolis. While the enamelled tiles of the colourful walls of Susa are more directly enchanting to the eye, it is the scale and monumental grandeur of Persepolis which allows us a glimpse of the richness of the lives led by these Persian monarchs at the height of the Empire. And yet, for all its glory, which may still be seen in the remnants which have survived, Persepolis is something of a mystery. It does not even stand on the Royal Road of the Persians which, at the height of Persian power, around 500 BC, ran from Sardis in Lydia, across what are now Turkey, Syria and Iraq, through to the city of Susa. Yet early every year the kings and their retinue would repair to this centre, which during the spring would appear to have been fully occupied.

Persepolis was probably founded by Cyrus himself, but the winged bull guardians carry a dedication by the mighty Xerxes, Darius's son, made to the god Ahura Mazda, which suggests that this king built the palace and several other important buildings. The Per-

Monumental stairway leading to the Apadana, or audience chamber, at Persepolis.

sian Apadana, or audience chamber, which is the best preserved of the remains in the centre, may be taken as an indication of the scale of the buildings at Persepolis. It is constructed on a base 2·7 metres (9 feet) high, and the main hall had a timber roof supported by thirty-six columns, each 19·5 metres (65 feet) tall, with double capitals mainly in the form of stylized bull heads. Its massive walls, which were originally painted in bright colours of a highly symbolic nature, were 5 metres (17 feet) thick, with enormous

PERSEPOLIS

A reconstruction of the Apadana at Persepolis, and a three-dimensional plan of the city. This is a vast audience chamber, the timber roof of which was supported by thirty-six columns, each 19.5 metres (65 feet) high, the whole building raised on a base 2.7 metres (9 feet) high. It has four enormous crenellated towers, one at each corner, which completed a basic span some 50 metres square. Leading up to the chamber is a monumental approach stairway which was designed to take mounted horses, and the flanking walls are decorated with sculptural reliefs depicting the various nations bringing tribute such as dromedaries and horses to the Persian king (right).

The reconstruction of the magnificent bull capitals of the Apadana (see opposite page) are based on substantial remains at Persepolis, and relate to Persian zodiac imagery. The bull of the Persians, which was the ancestor of Taurus in the modern zodiac, was linked with a fixed star now called Aldebaran, set in Taurus. This was one of the four prime stars of the Persians, one of the so-called 'Watchers of the Heavens', by which buildings were orientated. The image of the bull, raised high upon a column which connects it to the ground, symbolizes cosmic forces and their close relationship with the earth.

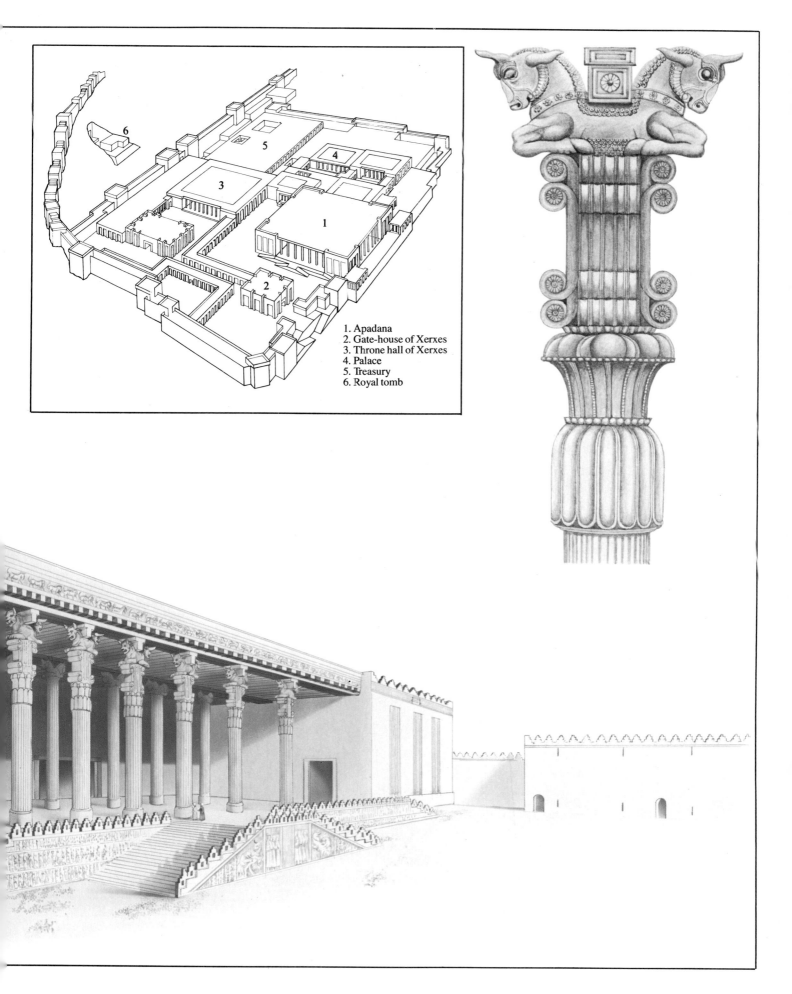

1. Apadana
2. Gate-house of Xerxes
3. Throne hall of Xerxes
4. Palace
5. Treasury
6. Royal tomb

Detail of bas-reliefs depicting a procession, on the stairway to the Apadana.

Little indeed is known about Persepolis – even the names conveniently appended to the various buildings by archaeologists are, except for the Apadana, a matter of informed guesswork, rather than of sure and certain knowledge.

The Apadana has a monumental double reversed stairway of 111 steps, designed with sufficient width and slope to allow horsemen to ascend. The focal point of the processional staircase is a raised winged disc, which is a symbolic form for the god of light, Ahura Mazda, reminding us that Herodotus, the Greek historian, insisted that 'the Persians did not have images of their gods in human forms as the Greeks do'. In a sense, however, Herodotus was wrong, for the human form of the god of the Zoroastrian religion of the Persians was in fact the body of the Persian king. In those days, as we find so often in widely different cultures in ancient times, kings were regarded as the embodiment of gods, themselves in direct contact with the spiritual world, the physical receptacle for divine power. Thus, the king was regarded as being in the service of the light-god Ahura Mazda (who ruled the light which came from the sun, rather than the sun itself, as is popularly supposed), and therefore eternally confronted the god of darkness and death, Angra Mainyu, who was also the spirit of lies.

It is evident from this cosmic relationship of the kings to the deities why they should regard their missions and military exploits as being concerned with the spreading of light and culture. Cyrus, for all his weight of men and arms, and expansionist Empire, was no mere strong-armed conqueror supported by a god, even in terms of contemporary propaganda. He was a cultured benefactor of those peoples who fell beneath his rule. The best of these kings were really intent on furthering the civilization of the god of light, who would militate against the darkness and lies which counter such civilization. This strong religious conviction explains why Cyrus did not impose a terrible yoke on those he conquered, and why he had great respect for the morals and customs of the divergent races within his Empire. The most popular memory of him, as the restorer of freedom to the Jews in Babylonian enslavement (as was actually predicted of Cyrus in the Jewish oracles), and as the king who permitted them to rebuild their temple in Jerusalem, which was under his

supporting corner towers, the whole structure being 50 metres (167 feet) square.

Especially beautiful, even today, are the sculptural remains of the stairway to the Apadana, reliefs which depict twenty-three different nations of the known world bringing tribute to the Persian king. Susa offers weapons and lions, the Babylonians bring cups and buffaloes, the Lydians, famous for their horsemanship, bring wonderful horses, and so on. Especially striking on these reliefs are the images of the animals, for the Persian artists (who appear to have had Greek artists working alongside them, perhaps captured in the wars), show an especially alert observation of nature, and a fine feeling for the plastic movement of the creatures. In contrast, the heavy drapery of the people, along with their formal military array and posture, seems to have precluded any real vitality entering into their images.

Persepolis once abounded in such relief sculpture. All the terraces and the kiln-dried brick walls were decorated with beautifully wrought figures, which were originally painted in rich colours. It now requires a real exercise of imagination to visualize this centre as it must have appeared. Persepolis has not yet been fully restored, or even completely explored by archaeologists. What survives shows that only such sections as the doorways, windows and columns were of stone, taken from the neighbouring limestone quarries. The wall spaces were built from dried mud bricks, which have in the intervening centuries fallen away, leaving the stonework standing somewhat like cropped-out teeth.

control, encapsulates a powerful moral about the nature of the Persian Empire at its finest.

As we stand amidst the ruins of Persepolis, we might well lament the loss of its former splendour, and indeed of the cultural impulse of which it was an outer sign. On the other hand, we might be consoled by the thought that we are lucky to have anything left at all after the alleged destruction of the centre at the hands of the soldiers of Alexander the Great, in 330 BC. Perhaps he saw the obliteration of Persepolis as the final demise of those hated Persians who had spoilt his own Greece and dealt in similar fashion with the buildings which stood on the Acropolis.

However, just as there is a mystery attached to the beginnings of Persepolis, so there is one in its ending. We are not absolutely certain about the supposed destruction by Alexander, and some historians deny the legendary accounts of a drunken orgy at the city's capture by the Greeks, and of its burning at the instigation of the courtesan Thais. It is said that medieval Islamic princes still used this palace up to the ninth century. What we do know is that until the last century Persepolis was only a heap of rubble in the desert.

Remains of one of the monumental gateways.

GREECE

View of the Acropolis in Athens, looking up
towards the Parthenon.

Knossos

One of the many legends connected with the island of Crete tells of a labyrinth, built by King Minos, in which was imprisoned a bull-headed monster called the Minotaur, which lived on the flesh of adolescents. When the archaeologist Sir Arthur Evans unearthed the ancient palace of Knossos in Crete, and observed the complexity of its fifteen hundred rooms, he announced quite solemnly that he had discovered this ancient labyrinth. However, he was almost certainly wrong – although somewhat complex in design, this is no labyrinth but a palace in which no Minotaur or Greek youth might lose himself permanently.

The palace itself is real enough, however, and even by modern standards it appears to have been luxurious, for it had complex water conduits and well-designed ventilation and drainage systems. It is ideally located upon a small hillside in a lovely landscape, about 4 kilometres (2½ miles) from the sea. It is said that, along with the inhabitants of the nearby port, the total population of the palace and its extensive precincts must have been nearly 100,000, making it the largest city in Europe in its day.

What greets the visitor to the ancient city of Knossos today is a work of substantial reconstruction, in which several buildings have been reassembled by Sir Arthur Evans to show the palace as he visualized it to be in around 1600 BC. It is built around a huge central courtyard, which facilitates communication between the many buildings, and gives access to light and air for ventilation. A western courtyard acts as a frontal precinct to the approach to the palace. The whole palace covers an area of 22,000 sq. metres (237,000 sq. feet), and there were almost certainly three storeys to the main palace on the west side, and five storeys to the east (not a particularly wise piece of design in an area liable to earthquakes). The chief apartments of the domestic area have a wonderful view over the east of the valley, and are flanked by a narrow courtyard. Next to these rooms is what is now known as the queen's *megaron*, or hall, although it quite possibly had nothing to do with the queen at all. On the other side of the central courtyard there is a broad staircase which originally led from an entrance hall up to the (now removed) state apartments. To the north was a long roadway (now used as part of the approach for tourists) which was apparently designed for receptions and ceremonials. This in turn leads into one of the most charming areas of the modern site, which is said to have been a theatre. It is almost certain that the dressed limestone was originally covered entirely in plaster and painted in bright colours, both inside and out.

The sanctuary and throne rooms have been reconstructed, and within the latter is a painted 'sacred griffin' which is surely no griffin but a composite creature with a lion's body, the head of an eagle, and a snake's tail. This figure is tantalizingly related to ancient mystery traditions which have been preserved in images in our own Old Testament, in the vision of Ezekiel. They also survive in the images of the four fixed signs of the zodiac and in the popular images of the symbols associated with the four apostles. Such survivals might well indicate that the palace centre at Knossos was, like many of the centres in Egypt and Greece, closely linked with the ancient mysteries through which the history and development of mankind was directed in early days.

If Sir Arthur Evans projected into history a myth (which is still widely believed) that placed the Minotaur beneath these walls, he also created a new history for Crete itself which was widely accepted by historians, but has now come into doubt. On the basis of supposed rebuilding needed as a result of wars or earthquakes, he gave this history three main divisions: the early, middle and

Aerial view of Knossos, the ancient palace-city of Crete, as restored by Sir Arthur Evans.

late Minoan periods. The early Minoan period was the thousand years up to 2000 BC, the middle Minoan some four centuries, up to 1600 BC, and the late Minoan a short period up to 1250 BC, after which the palace and its precincts appear to have been deserted. Evans also suggested an earlier proto-Minoan period of some ten millennia, but this has been hotly disputed and much corrected, so that it is now accepted as being less than half Evans's estimate. Nevertheless, it is still regarded by some as marking the beginning of European civilization.

The Golden Age of Knossos was around 1600 BC, commencing with the so-called 'New Palace' period, and during these years the king, as commander of a huge fleet, appears to have ruled over much of the Mediterranean. To judge from the surviving records, and from the hints afforded by artistic remains, a pleasant life was enjoyed.

Unfortunately, one only has to see through the praise lavished upon this site by tourist boards and travel agents, to realize just how uninteresting to a serious historian the site as it stands really is. Much of the 'restoration' put in hand under the direction of Evans is tasteless in the extreme, and one feels, for example, that a more appropriate material than reinforced concrete could have been used for this purpose. On a more academic level, many of his restorations are based more on guesswork than upon certainty of fact, and the paintings which have been 'restored' or placed in the complex of rooms are of a poor standard, and suggest nothing of true Minoan art. In a sense, Evans and his team have smothered the real feeling of Knossos by removing those delicate nuances, found in the majority of ancient sites, which enable the imaginative visitor to see with the eyes of the spirit what might once have been there. One may indeed gain more conception of the greatness of Knossos in the Museum at Heraklion than on the Evans site itself. Here, in the Museum, are the remains of pottery, of ancient scripts, toys, and familiar household utensils which speak more eloquently than the restorations a few kilometres away.

To judge from the surviving images on seals and paintings, the women wore long gowns with small aprons, the top having

The precinct of the ancient palace at Knossos.

short sleeves and leaving the breasts provocatively exposed. Among the paintings which have partly survived are so-called 'bull-dancers', which depict one or more young men and women teasing bulls, sometimes leaping over their horns. No one is sure what these scenes represent, although they were probably connected with religious rites.

Evans postulated that the Minoan culture was destroyed by earthquake. In his digging he found certain indications that the palace had been deserted in a hurry, and indeed his theory was dramatically supported in 1926, when he was personally supervising the restoration, for the island suffered an enormous earth tremor which destroyed many buildings in nearby Heraklion. However, as with so much when one looks at this ancient site, no one is quite sure how the city came to be abandoned, nor exactly what the life was like that went on there, and Knossos has been subject to more speculation than almost any other site in the Mediterranean. Some people have postulated that the legend of Atlantis refers to Crete, that the story told by Plato of a fabulous civilization being engulfed by the sea derives from a memory of the sudden destruction of the Minoan world by some natural catastrophe.

Other legends, too, accrue to the palace. Its architect, and designer of the labyrinth, was held by the Greeks to be the famed Daedalus. Having argued with King Minos, Daedalus and his son Icarus had to flee the island, and did so by flying with wings made of feathers and wax. Icarus flew too close to the sun and plunged into the ocean when his wings melted. This familiar story, and the many other legends attached to Knossos, show what fascination the place had for the Greeks, and testify to the existence of a once powerful and sophisticated civilization.

Mycenae

The megalithic gateway, often called the 'Lion Gate'.

Mycenae is a fortified hilltop, about 10 kilometres (6 miles) from Argos, near another related hill citadel of Tiryns. It is by far the oldest city in Greece, and one of the most important of the prehistoric civilizations in the area. The Mycenaeans who settled this area, perhaps in 2000 BC, were Homer's 'Achaeans', the earliest of the Greek-speaking people known to us, and they appear to have had, especially through their productive relationship with Crete, an inestimable effect on the development of early European civilization.

The recovery of this ancient culture is almost entirely due to the dreams and work of one man, the German Heinrich Schliemann, one of the most remarkable figures of the nineteenth century – a self-made millionaire, an erudite linguist (he claimed that he could learn a new language in six weeks), with a lifelong dream of proving Homer's writings to be more than mere fantasy. Schliemann, who had previously been one of the main influences behind the discovery of the ancient site of Troy, was convinced that the 'Greek' army which rose against Troy was from Mycenae, and that it was here that King Agamemnon was murdered by his wife, who had been as faithless to their marriage as the king himself. Schliemann's work at Mycenae, which started in 1876, led not only to the discovery of incredible treasures of gold and works of art, but also to conclusive proof that this had been the home and burial place of the historical Atreids of Greek literature.

Schliemann developed his intuitions by following his conviction that the literary texts of the ancients were accurate, even in those cases where they contradicted modern scientific hypotheses. In this way he amassed a vast knowledge about the nature of the original sites (admittedly at times with a somewhat ham-fisted archaeological method) as well as great treasures and works of art.

With typical panache, he wrote of his Mycenaean discoveries, 'All the museums of the world taken together do not have one fifth as much', but this of course was before the discoveries of the riches in the tomb of Tutankhamen. The wealth which Schliemann recovered from these tombs was derived from the fact that the Mycenaean kings were middlemen on a huge scale, for their cities were well placed on the trade routes from the islands to the mainland, on those routes which led to Europe proper.

Schliemann's ideas and methods earned him a scarcely deserved bad reputation among the European *savants* and academic experts in the fields upon which his amateurism encroached, and one brilliant comment by the archaeologist C. W. Ceram is a sort of kindly epitaph to the work of this great German: 'The professional's mistrust of the successful outsider is the mediocrity's mistrust of the genius.' Much of the Schliemann treasure was 'lost' during the last war, the tale being told in Ceram's extraordinary collection of archaeological stories of the past, *Gods, Graves and Scholars*. Fortunately, many of Schliemann's finds are preserved securely in the National Museum in Athens.

'I have gazed upon the face of Agamemnon' is the text of the cable which Schliemann is supposed to have sent to the King of Greece in 1876, after he had discovered in a tomb, under a gold mask, the preserved face of an ancient Mycenaean, obviously of royal blood. In fact, what Schliemann did say in this telegram was less dramatic, but similarly connected with the ancient legends of Greece, for he reported the discovery of the graves of Agamemnon, Cassandra and their comrades 'all killed during the banquet by Clytemnestra and her lover, Aegisthus'. In the event, Schliemann's love for the literature of the ancient Greeks led him astray, for the tombs later proved to be even earlier than the time of Agamemnon, who was murdered in 1240 BC: these burials were about 300 years older than this. However, the name has stuck, and even to this day, a gold grave-mask in the National Museum is called the 'mask of Agamemnon', while one of the buildings at Mycenae is named after that king, another after his father Atreus.

It has been suggested (rather unconvincingly, in my opinion) that the golden masks found in the royal burials at Mycenae were actual portraits of the deceased. Certainly very few of these masks could be regarded as being portraits in the modern sense of the word, for they are too stylized. On the other hand, it is certain that in a few cases, especially in several child burials, the mask was made by pressing a sheet of gold-leaf over the dead face, thus obtaining a direct impression. The hands and feet of the children were also wrapped in gold-leaf. This practice may well be the origin of the ancient Roman custom of preserving waxen portrait masks of their ancestors in the *atrium* of their homes.

The best-known building at Mycenae is known as the Treasury of Atreus, which is one of several beehive burial chambers at the site – although it does happen to be the finest and the most beautifully preserved. It was built about 1400 BC, of ashlar, and is 30 metres (100 feet) in diameter inside, and 14 metres (47 feet) high at the apex, being built up from a series of thirty-five rings of heavy stones which were smoothed down after being laid. As an enclosed space under a rotunda, this was not surpassed in size or design until Hadrian built the Pantheon

A gold burial mask found in one of the tombs by Heinrich Schliemann, now in the National Museum, Athens.

nearly fifteen hundred years later! The whole of this beehive form was constructed below ground, under a hill, and then the outer entrance was built so as to allow an approach by a walled passageway (a *dromos*) about 35 metres (115 feet) long and 6 metres (21 feet) wide. The actual burial was not within the beehive, but inside a chamber cut into the rock-face from the beehive. The inside of the beehive was originally decorated with metal friezes and frescoes which covered the corbelled construction.

The entrance was flanked with columns bearing chevron patterns, and part of these eventually found their way to the British Museum by way of Ireland, having been 'collected' by an over-zealous Victorian tourist. The lintel over the door is made of two enormous stones, the inner one alone weighing 120 tonnes, which helps to explain why the later Greeks claimed that these structures were built by the Cyclops, the one-eyed giants of their legends. The fact that these buildings are on such a large scale has led one or two archaeologists and historians to suggest that Stonehenge in England was built either by Mycenaeans, or by people who had learned the art of building within their culture. However, Stonehenge is probably much older than the Mycenaean civilization and those attested traces of Mycenaean or Mediterranean designs in Stonehenge, and in the burials there, might well have been added much later.

The entrance to the circuit of citadel walls is a gate usually called the 'Lion Gate'. In fact, it is almost certainly a lioness-gate, to judge from later records, and from surviving impression seals relating to Mycenaean culture. It was constructed about 1260 BC, and, like the tombs, the walls it is set in appear to have been built by giants. In this case, the lintel supporting the two headless lionesses is some 5 metres (16 feet) long by 1 metre (3 feet) high at its middle point, and 2·4 metres (8 feet) deep. The significance of the lionesses which stand rampant is unknown, but they may have had a connection with kingship.

From this gateway there is a long ramp which leads up to a high court area. Almost certainly the palace of the historical Agamemnon once stood here, whose family and treasures the archaeologist Heinrich Schliemann sought so assiduously.

Below The processional entrance to the beehive tomb which is known as the Treasury of Atreus. *Right* Site of the circle of royal burials, beyond the 'Lion Gate'. *Below right* Cross-section and plan of the Treasury of Atreus. The *dromos* is to the right of the plan and the burial chamber at 90 degrees to it, off the 'beehive'.

Delphi

Delphi's oracle, famed throughout the Classical world, lies somewhere in the shady areas between myth and reality, owing as much to the work of the gods as to the earthly aspirations of men. When Hercules consulted the oracle in order to see how he could make amends for terrible crimes, he was set the task for which we still remember him – the twelve labours. Yet Hercules, like Oedipus and Orestes who also sought their blighted destinies in Delphi, belongs mainly to the realm of myth, and may scarcely be placed in time. Xerxes, on the other hand, was a very time-bound person, with the entire weight of Persia on his imperial shoulders. In his rage at the Greeks, and in his greed, he sent soldiers to loot this holy centre. When they reached the Temple of Athena, however, they were met by terrible thunderstorms and an avalanche – in their eyes an obvious sign that the gods were angered – and so they turned back, with the result that the damage done by the Persians to Athens was not done to Delphi. Later, however, the Romans were more successful, for Sulla plundered it, and later Nero stole some five hundred bronze statues, not from greed, it is said, but from pique that the oracle should have condemned him for having murdered his mother!

Delphi was ancient even to the Persians and the Romans. It was old even when Homer wrote about the Pythia at Delphi, and was as far removed in time from Plato and Aristotle as the Battle of Hastings is from us. It is therefore hardly surprising that its origins should merge into shades of half-truth and myth.

For at least fourteen centuries before the birth of Christ, Delphi had been the goal of a constant stream of visitors and pilgrims in search of advice, or of predictions of the future, ranging from complex questions of state to less momentous personal matters. Delphi's priestess, the Pythia, would enter a

The Tholos, a circular temple, built around 400 BC.

deep trance (a 'divine frenzy') and make contact with invisible spirits with the power to foretell the future, which they would do through the medium of different voices which emanated from her. It was the most important of all Greek oracles, and has been seen by historians as one of the great undisturbed points of stability in the turbulent history of the ancient world, revered even by the enemies of Greece.

The method of consulting the oracle has inevitably been romanticized and dramatized by later writers, but as far as it is possible to tell it appears to have been fairly simple, although obviously deeply involved with sacred rituals and mysteries of which modern man has no understanding. The questions were given in writing to male priests by the petitioner, and these were then submitted to the priestess. She then entered the sacred shrine (the *adyton*), took her seat on the sacred golden tripod (removed by an early Christian Emperor), chewed bay leaves, drank from a goblet of spring water (drawn from the River Cassotis), and then entered a trance. She was regarded by the priests as being in direct contact with the spiritual world whilst in such a trance, and therefore with access to profound wisdom. The reply given from this trance-state was passed on (often in an edited form) to the petitioner, who would have made some suitable gift to the oracle. Very often the oracle's answer was put into a hexametric verse.

The divine frenzy which caused the sibyls to make their predictions at Delphi was said to be connected with the powerful forces arising from that area of the earth itself. A lone goatherd, so the story goes, was supposed to have chanced upon the spot, whereupon he was driven into a frenzy, along with one of his goats, and inspired to make prophecies. Others drawn there were also beguiled in this way, and so it became clear that the place was beset by strange forces from the earth. Not surprisingly, it was soon associated with the Earth goddess Gaea, and regarded as the *omphalos,* the navel of the world. After some hundred years this goddess was partly dispossessed by the Sun-god Apollo, with the advent of the race of Dorians (about 1100 BC), and as these people, the real founders of Greece, prospered, Delphi reached its peak of fortune.

Others deny this early history, and say that it was chosen not by a goatherd, but by Zeus himself through the flight of his eagles. It is indeed easy to see this exquisite scenery as something painted by a god, with the green slopes of the majestic Parnassus rolling down to the deep blue of the sea far below. It is a setting, as Lord Byron put it, born 'in the phrensy of a dreamer's eye'.

The earth of the mountains, and the water of the sea below, are combined in the particular name given to the god Apollo when speaking through the Pythia. Apollo was the Sun-god, and shone on this place in the same way that the sun itself shines to this day, but he was called *Apollo delphinios,* a name which brings together associations of water and ancient earth forces as *delphis* means 'dolphin' and *delphys* means 'womb'. In both name and legend we find Delphi deeply rooted in the spiritual world which supported and sustained Greek culture in those lands for a thousand years or so, and which continues to echo even in our own time, two thousand years later.

The Greek *temenos* was the 'sacred precinct', which usually included a sacred grove of trees, a temple and shrines, as well as places designed for quiet reflection and meditation. In some cases, as for example in the Acropolis in Athens, the tenemos was built in a raised and well-defended place, to make it a sort of holy citadel. The one in Delphi was built along similar lines, for here we have not only the temples and shrines, but also a theatre, used for an eight-year cycle of music festivals, and three treasuries – the Cnidian, which was built in 565 BC, the Siphnian, built in 530 BC (with lovely caryatid columns), and the Athenian treasury of 510 BC. This latter was built in an extensive rebuilding programme which included the Doric Temple of Apollo (the earlier one being destroyed by an earthquake), and the beautiful theatre. There was also a stadium used for an eight-year cycle of games and religious festivals.

Within the treasuries were immense riches made up of offerings to the oracle – the historian Pliny tells us that he counted three thousand statues alone, and this was after the thefts of Nero and others. Some of these works of art are now in the Museum at Delphi. None surpasses the magnificent Charioteer of Sotades, made in the fifth century, which may be regarded as the human

counterpart of the statue to Poseidon in Athens.

Delphi is now much restored, and like all ancient places in Greece, a centre of a different kind of pilgrimage, though the tourists flock to it with the same insistence, and perhaps even with the same questions, as the visitors of previous ages. Their questions remain unanswered, however, for the place no longer works its ancient magic. When Julian, the Emperor of Rome who tried to turn back the tides of Christianity in favour of the ancient mysteries, decided to restore the oracle at Delphi, he first made inquiries of it. The oracle paid attention to his question, but it was answered only with a statement that the oracle was to remain silent in the future, as though this last means of access to the spiritual world had been withdrawn from mankind by the very gods themselves.

The portico to the Athenian treasury, where many of the rich offerings to the oracle were kept.

Paestum

When the poet Shelley wrote of the perfection of Greek art he had never visited Greece, and knew its art mainly through Roman copies. But he may have seen the magnificent Doric temples in southern Italy, at Paestum, products of the colonial impulse of Greek civilization at the height of its power. These buildings alone are sufficiently magnificent to confirm Shelley's feeling that with the demise of Greek perfection in art, something had been lost forever.

Greek art is the art of balance. Strong, almost heavy, horizontals are met by the thrust of fragile columns, and the whole sits

Below The Temple of Poseidon at Paestum, perhaps the best preserved of Doric temples.

Above Life-size bronze statue of Poseidon (the sea-god of the Greeks), now in the National Museum, Athens.

straight and firm, defying disturbance. This perfect Greek balance may still be experienced in the exquisite Doric temples at Paestum in southern Italy. One is dedicated to Poseidon, the god of the sea, another to Demeter, the earth goddesss, and the third – the so-called 'basilica' – is of unknown dedication, but was certainly built in the late sixth century.

The most beautiful of these three temples is that of Poseidon, which was built about 460 BC. Not only is this the finest of the Greek buildings in Italy, but it is in some ways the best preserved of all Doric temples. As with the Parthenon on the Acropolis, there are two ranges of columns, forming three aisles. The columns were constructed in two tiers, as is obvious from the surviving temple structure. The roof would originally have been covered with tiles, probably in Paestum with marble tiles. The supporting columns are 9 metres (29 feet) high, with a diameter at their lower thickness of 2 metres (6 ft 9 in). Within the inner columns of this temple, the Naos, the principal chamber in the Greek temples, is almost complete. The word Naos meant 'dwelling-place', and it was used by the priests of the temples to indicate that the god to whom the temple was dedicated might at certain times live within that area. Votive statues were kept there, perhaps to encourage this 'incarnation' of the god. In this particular

View through the interior of the Temple of Poseidon.

temple at Paestum there would have been a large statue of Poseidon, wielding his trident, perhaps rather like the one on the next page.

This design reflects something of the nature of the Greek approach to worship, for the inner area marked off by the inner columns would have been accessible only to priests, and it is indeed very likely that only highly favoured individuals would have been allowed to walk even in the outer galleries, from which they might have been able to catch a glimpse of the votive statue within. The general public would scarcely have been allowed within the temple at all, on the principle that it was the home of the gods, and the centre for the ancient religious rituals and mysteries.

The magnificent figure depicted here was recovered from beneath Poseidon's own waves in 1928, north of Euboea, and now invigorates the atmosphere of one of the large exhibition halls in the National Museum,

Athens. It has been suggested that this bronze statue, which stands 2·09 metres (6 ft 11 in) high, was stolen by the Romans from a temple, and the god took revenge at this outrage and sank the thieving boat. While there is every reason to doubt that this Poseidon bronze should ever have stood in Paestum, the statue was made at about the same time as the temple was built, that is, around 450 BC, and it is not unreasonable to imagine that a very similar figure once graced the interior of the Paestum temple.

It is in some ways fitting that the Temple of Poseidon and that of Demeter should be together at Paestum, for the very name Poseidon meant 'Husband of the goddess Da'. This latter name was one of those used by Demeter, the earth goddess, and unfortunate mother of the lovely Persephone, who was condemned to spend four months of each year in the dark underworld ruled by Hades, the Greek equivalent of Pluto. The dedica-

tion to such gods might remind us that the rituals involved the Greeks in a worship orientated towards sunrise – exactly the opposite of the westward-looking priests of later Christian worship. This is reflected in the simple external forms of the Greek religion – as opposed to the sacred 'mysteries' conducted inside the temple – which were performed on the steps, in the open air, in full view of those participating outside the temple and directed towards the rising sun. This precise orientation is preserved at Paestum. Since it was believed that all the gods were in some direct way connected with Helios, the sun, they were therefore seen as streaming towards the earth from this direction in the first morning light.

Paestum itself has very well-preserved walls, 4·5 kilometres (almost 3 miles) in circumference, made from local limestone blocks. These three temples were also made from a coarse local limestone (unlike those on the Greek mainland, for which a fine marble would have been used), and, in order to obtain the desired quality of finish and colour, they were covered with a fine marble stucco of marble mixed with plaster.

Paestum has other archaeological interest besides the three Greek temples. During the construction of a runway and aerodrome in the Second World War the remains of a large neolithic cemetery were discovered, which indicates that the site was an important one long before the Greeks colonized the area, probably because of its position on the Gulf of Salerno. After the Greeks, the Romans developed the town further, with the result that there is one large ruin of a Roman temple, as well as the almost inevitable amphitheatre, a market centre, and town hall, along with many houses and tombs. But even with the later Roman settlement it is to the Greek genius that this Italian site bears witness.

The Acropolis

The high plateau of the Acropolis in Athens was a fortified stronghold long before the Greeks came to the area (parts of the Mycenaean fortifications are still visible), but it is the work of the Greeks of the fifth century which amazes those who come to the Acropolis in modern times. This ancient Athens was that of the leader Pericles, a city of some quarter of a million people – a democracy based on human slavery – so imbued with the religious spirit that all roads led to the holy buildings on this hilltop. In a war against the Greeks, which they lost finally, but in which they won some of the battles, Persian armies had destroyed the temple on the Acropolis in 480 BC, so Pericles commissioned the great artist Phidias to head a team of architects in the design of a new and splendid home for their goddess, Athena Parthenos, 'the Virgin'. The result was the Parthenon, the largest temple in the Acropolis, which also includes a smaller temple, known as the Erechtheum, and the Propylaea, the entrance hall. Although the Parthenon is now only partly standing, it is still wholly serene, in a beauteous harmony of proportions.

The caryatid porch of the Erechtheum, which stands on the Acropolis in Athens. The second caryatid on the left is a copy, the original having been removed by Lord Elgin.

Some of the secrets which Phidias incorporated into this dwelling for Athena are secrets no longer. We know that the distance between the columns and the column-diameter was in a ratio of 9:4, the very ratio which runs through the whole building – for example, it marks the length to the breadth of the structure, the width to the height, and so on. There were subtle variations on the straight line expected of architecture in order to allow for minute compensations natural to the human eye. For example, the sides of the columns swell outwards in what the Greeks called *entasis*, which counteracts the visual distortion whereby load-bearing columns normally appear to curve inwards in the middle. A more subtle adjustment was made with the angle of the columns to the vertical: they are so orientated to the plumb vertical that the extension of their central lines would meet together at a point high above the building. Such a subtle arrangement was made in order to correct the distortion natural to human vision, the inference being that the merely human was not good enough for a house dedicated to Athena. A list of other similar ratios and adjustments could be made but is unnecessary, for the simple truth is that all this sophistication of measurement is valid only because it works: we look at this building and we see perfection.

Phidias is usually credited with the work of sculpture on the pediment, but this was too vast an enterprise for one man. A frieze of reliefs 155 metres (512 feet) in length would be too much at a time when he was busy working on the 12-metre (40-foot) freestanding statue of Athena intended for the sanctum, and so he employed a whole studio of brilliant men. Thanks to the guile of Lord Elgin, many of these sculptures are safe from the exhaust fumes of Athens, being lodged in the British Museum.

The marble perfection of the Parthenon (painted in beautiful but bright colours which might disturb us nowadays) was ready for dedication in 438 BC. The Roman writer Plutarch said that while the Acropolis was built in a short time, it was built for eternity, 'as though the buildings were animated with a spirit of perpetual youth and unfading elegance'. This is as true now as it was in the days of Plutarch. Yet it is not merely the remains of the Acropolis architecture that impress us – it is that indefinable thing which

is as real as the marble itself, the spirit of the place.

When the Christian Emperor Theodosius closed down the pagan sanctuaries of Rome and Greece in AD 393, the Parthenon was changed overnight into a church, and the female tutelary spirit was renamed Mary, in the hope that the guardian force which had guided the Greeks through adversity and victory would now continue to protect the Christians. But some few centuries later the Parthenon sprouted a minaret, part of which is still visible, for it became a mosque, and served another God. Later the God of War was evoked, for in 1687 it was used as a storage chamber for the Turkish gunpowder, and in a single act of desecration (unparalleled perhaps until similar occurrences in the Second World War), a Venetian soldier quite intentionally fired a well-aimed shot into the Parthenon, and blew out its side.

To the north of the Parthenon, however, the Erechtheum is still standing. It has the most beautiful Ionic order capitals to be found in Greece, but probably its best-known feature is its six female statues, known as caryatids, which act as columns on the south porch. It was built in 421 BC, and has a history as complex and rich as the Parthenon itself. Having been used already as a treasury and reliquary, it was even pressed into service once as the harem of the Turkish rulers!

The remains of the Propylaea, which forms the entrance to the Acropolis, and which was built at the same time as the Parthenon.

THE ACROPOLIS

The general appearance of the Acropolis in the fifth century BC, looking over to the Parthenon from the north-west. Dominating the site, with its frontal porch looking directly with an unimpeded view over old Athens below, is the Parthenon. The complex of buildings to the bottom right of the reconstruction consists of the imposing entrance to the Acropolis, the Propylaea, and behind this a temple to Athena Nike. To the central left is the Erechtheum, on the far side of which is the famous caryatid porch.

The Parthenon was designed and constructed under the direction of the architect and sculptor Phidias, on the order of Pericles, and was dedicated to Athena Parthenos on completion in 438 BC. Phidias employed the architects Ictinus and Callicrates to help him, and established an entire workshop of highly skilled masons and sculptors.

The Propylaea was completed in 432 BC, and was designed by the architect Mnesicles, on a site which required great ingenuity of design, for it united the steep ascent of the Acropolis hill with a sharp cliff-face which led to the flat plateau of the *temenos* (the religious precinct) itself. The fact that the design is not symmetrical has suggested to some historians that the Propylaea was never completely finished because of financial and other restrictions imposed upon the Athenians by the Peloponnesian War. The dignity of its design was marred by Roman additions.

It is certain, on the other hand, that the asymmetrical design of the Erechtheum was intentional: it was constructed on two levels and with three interestingly related porches, two of which are visible in the reconstruction, the other being the caryatid porch. The curious design was adopted because the building was intended to replace a more ancient temple of Athena which had been damaged by the invading Persians, incorporating some of the religious elements of the original temple, as well as one or two important and highly venerated areas upon the Acropolis.

The western porch of the Erechtheum fronts on to a sacred area which overlaid the ground plan of the original temple of Athena (visible in the reconstruction as a sort of walled precinct). To the west of this stood a huge statue of Athena which could be seen from Athens below the Acropolis. There were also a number of sacred areas, temples to minor deities, and a few sacred groves within the temenos. The walls, which gave both protection and structure to the plateau of the Acropolis, followed much the same course as in modern times – indeed, certain of the pre-Grecian stones, relating to the more ancient Mycenaean cultures, may still be seen. Below the southern walls, which run along a steep façade of rocks and caves, there is a well-restored Theatre of Dionysus, the Asclepeum and the Odeon of Herodes Atticus. Connecting this latter with the Theatre of Dionysus is the Stoa, or detached colonnade, of Eumenes.

In the rocks of the cliff-face in the foreground there were several sacred areas, including a Cave of Apollo and a Cave of Pan, venerated by the later Greeks and Romans. In this area there was also a communal *clepshydra* – a water clock, used as a way of measuring time.

ROME

Leptis Magna – the remains of a well-preserved
Roman city in modern Libya, on the North
African coast.

Pompeii

In early Roman times twenty-two kilometres (about fourteen miles) south-east of Naples stood the small town of Pompeii, which sprang into renewed life in the second century BC, when Rome extended her martial diplomacy eastward. This town died, three centuries later, first under the impact of an earthquake, in AD 63, which destroyed many of its buildings, and then finally under the terrible eruption of the volcano Vesuvius, which had long been thought to be inactive.

The eruption was a dramatic affair, and was described by eye-witnesses, among the most famous of whom was Pliny the Younger, who had the thankless task of reporting the death of his uncle, Pliny the Elder, who had died under the volcano whilst attempting to rescue friends.

It took only two days of eruption for the town to be completely buried to a depth of about 6 metres (20 feet) beneath layers of pumice dust and ashes. Most of the population of 20,000 managed to escape, but a few hundred were caught in the acrid poisonous smoke and gases which centuries later were still to trouble archaeologists digging the site, for small volumes of it were trapped in pockets beneath the ashes. The result is that many skeletons have been found in the ruins, usually the bodies of those who hid in cellars, waiting for the eruption to cease, or of those who could not escape – as, for example, sixty-three gladiators near the arena who were shackled by the ankles. Other victims have received a somewhat rigid resurrection, for modern archaeological techniques have made it possible for the empty spaces formerly occupied by the decomposed bodies to be filled with plaster, so that we may now see the forms of these unfortunates, caught trying to escape, covering their faces with cloths or cushions, sometimes protecting children, huddling together, or even alone in their undignified *rigor mortis*.

Over a period of two hundred years, at first in an amateurish way, but more recently with increased sophistication in the archaeological methods, the town has been slowly dug out of the ashes, until only about a quarter of it still remains buried. A beautiful town in ruins is now open for our study, and for a moment or two of quiet reflection on the uncertainty of human life and aspirations – it is a ghost town where one may hear, in the imagination, the laughter and tears of a long-dead people. There are, indeed, few more poignant remains than those at Pompeii, which give an intimate picture of the life-style of an average Roman citizen.

The public buildings which have been dug out from the debris are loosely grouped into three areas: the forum, paved with huge stones and a double storey of colonnades,

Detail of a marble mask which decorated the fountain in one of the houses of Pompeii.

82

built to the west, near the sea; a group of temples, including one to Zeus Meilichius, and one to the Egyptian goddess Isis (though other temples are found scattered around the town, for example a large one in the forum area, dedicated to Jupiter, Juno and Minerva); and to the south-east the amphitheatre and the *palaestra*, intended for gymnastics and athletics. As always in Roman towns, Pompeii had several public baths, including the Stabian baths, which were built about 120 BC, and the Forum baths, built some forty years later.

The streets are still paved in the Roman manner, in places deeply incised with the wheel marks of the heavy traffic. It has been possible to identify familiar types of shop: bakeries with their ovens, taverns, inns, restaurants, and the equivalent of the modern 'snack bar', where a Roman in a hurry could perch on a stool for a rapid meal. Of the city's two theatres, one was open to the sky, and would accommodate up to 5000 spectators; behind it stood a huge training school for gladiators where the chained skeletons were later found. A much smaller and roofed theatre was probably intended for musical performances, rather than for theatrical pre-

The Temple of Isis, dedicated to the Egyptian goddess who was extremely popular among the many mystery cults adopted by the Romans.

The remains of the amphitheatre – this is the oldest surviving of all Roman arenas. Unlike the famous Colosseum in Rome, this arena has no subterranean rooms.

sentations, and this seated some 1500 people. Both these theatres are well preserved to this day, but many of the decorations and statues were removed during the two centuries of digging.

The amphitheatre, always the most popular centre for Roman entertainment, was built about 70 BC, and is actually the oldest surviving of all Roman amphitheatres. It was the scene of countless pageants and wild animal 'hunts', of gladiatorial games, and of public executions of convicted criminals. It is not likely, however, that Christians were put to death here, since the town was destroyed before the new religion took a strong hold on the Roman Empire.

Outside the town lay the roads and tombs. Roman law forbade burial inside city confines, with the result that tombs lined the main road leading from the town gates. The so-called 'Street of the Dead' in Pompeii, which leads from the fine triple gate of Herculaneum, is typical, for the tombs alongside

are often very elaborate and beautiful. One of the finest is that of Naevoleia Tyche, which was virtually a family chapel, with a marble-faced altar. As the Romans practised cremation, as well as earth-burial, several cinerary urns have been found there. (Incidentally, the law which prevented burials within cities explains why Christian catacomb burials were outside the original walls of Rome.)

It is not so much from the public buildings, as from the rather sad private remains of Pompeii that we are able to picture imaginatively how the ordinary citizens of such a town would live, nearly two thousand years ago. The houses have been discovered much as they had been deserted, with all the ordinary objects used for living still intact. A typical house comprised two main sections – the *atrium*, which was a sort of dignified formal living room, and the *peristyle* (behind the atrium), which was a more intimate family quarter, an inner garden, with statues,

fountains and a cloistered walk. These two central areas had rooms built off them, and since the doors and unglazed windows looked on to these central parts, a perfect privacy was ensured for those who lived within.

These private houses were often surrounded by shops and workshops, built into the walls of the houses themselves. The floors were decorated with mosaics, the walls painted with frescoes. The most remarkable of such pictures are the wonderful murals found in the large Villa of the Mysteries (a villa so enormous that there are over sixty rooms downstairs alone), just outside Pompeii. The subjects of these murals are connected with the ancient mystery cults and initiation ceremonies which were part of the cult of the god Dionysus.

The kitchens in these small houses were behind the peristyle, usually looking out on to a garden, and with a separate back entrance. The houses were originally heated by ducted warm air – a most efficient method of central heating in a slave society where labour was very cheap – fed from individual furnaces below ground level.

If we were to imagine a small modern city or town, perhaps by the seaside, with a population of about 20,000 people, being miraculously preserved some two thousand years into the future, we may realize how unlikely it is that the houses and objects found within them would measure up to the quality of those found in Pompeii. The standard of workmanship – even to judge from the objects which have survived a long period of systematic removal – is extraordinary, and it indicates that the Romans surrounded themselves with art almost as a necessity of life, rather than a luxury. Many of the lovely objects which have been found by responsible archaeologists in these houses, for example, lamps, vases, statues, plates, and so on, have been displayed in the museums at Naples and in Pompeii: some of them astonish with their sheer beauty.

The Colosseum

The Roman architect Vitruvius insisted that public architecture should unite in a single form the three 'virtues' of beauty, solidity and utility, and the Colosseum, built in the same century in which Vitruvius lived, was designed to demonstrate exactly such a unity.

We are nowadays accustomed to seeing aerial photographs of the Colosseum – pictures which reveal it to be something like a deep oval dish, with vertical sides, and with what appears to be the remains of a labyrinth in the central area. The Romans for whom this enormous pile was constructed never saw it like that. Outside it, they were overawed by its size from below, and once inside they had other things to think about than the building itself, since their attention was directed to the spectacular entertainment of the day.

The central area was not a labyrinth, but a flat space covered with what the Romans called *arena* – sand – which was sprinkled there to soak up the blood of those unfortunates who provided the entertainment. Beneath this sanded area was indeed a network of corridors and rooms, but this was no maze – merely a well-designed system for caging wild beasts and people. Within this network there was an ingenious lift system, run by a complex manipulation of counterweights, which would lift the various human and animal victims to the arena above. Here were also the water ducts by which the engineers might flood parts of the arena for vast mock naval battles (*naumachia*).

The true genius of the Roman architect lay in his ability to use concrete, and this is put to great effect within the amphitheatre, even though the structure itself is built using stone arches. It is 186 by 154 metres (620 by 513 feet), the seats being ranged in vertical walls 47 metres (157 feet) high. This vast ellipse of stone blocks, slabs and marble, which measures 84 by 52 metres (280 by 175 feet) internally, rests firmly on a concrete 'footing' some 7 metres (25 feet) thick! A unified ring

of stone, it is separated from the arena by a wall nearly 4 metres (13 feet) high, the whole being faced in a fine quality marble, which was removed in the Middle Ages. This must have been a magnificent sight in its pristine condition.

The very name Colosseum, however, raises images of gladiators fighting to the death, of the wild roars of animals mutilated or mutilating, the screams of the dying. Even today no great imagination is required within these walls to feel the presence of subhuman evil. Estimates vary somewhat, but it seems fairly certain that the Colosseum could hold over

55,000 people, rank upon rank, within its walls, so that they might look down in comparative comfort on the agonies of the person, or of the few hundred people, below. One may only speculate on what went through the minds of such people then – perhaps they felt secure in their seats (for more than one writer has insisted that the entertainments were linked with religious rituals), or perhaps they secretly wondered when it might be their turn to be on the inside of that sand-strewn pit.

The building of the Colosseum began under Vespasian in AD 70, and took some twelve years to complete. Even now, for all the feeling of black magic it evokes, and even in its ruin, the structure is noble. It is certainly doubtful whether any building has ever been erected with such devotion to such an idea – that human beings and animals be confined in one place, yet out of sight, to be conveniently ducted to meet their deaths at a central point where they can be watched by thousands. Certainly the utility of the triad eulogized by Vitruvius is well satisfied here, even if one doubts that a stone extermination centre (placed in the middle of a city which was then the war-centre of the world) could ever be really beautiful.

Inside the tall outer ring of linked stone arches were ranged the marble tiers which held wooden seats (both marble and wood having been removed long ago), with each separate level designated for a different rank, as one would expect in a world where rank was more carefully distinguished than it is today. Nearest to the arena, occupying the first two rows, were the boxes and seats reserved for the emperor, and for the higher ranks of officials. Even the entrances themselves were 'graded', for of the eighty archways, four were private to the emperor, with special triumphal gateways. In this way, the natural pyramid of social order, which would picture the god-king at the top, is inverted, for the hordes of the poorest members of the society are positioned above, and further away from the spectacle.

This inner disorder of the pyramid is mocked on the outside, for there the simplest Doric order – the salt of the architectural earth – is used on the lower of the three levels of 240 arches, whilst the more sophisticated Corinthian is used at the top. This has led some travellers to see something symbolic in the architecture, but the fact is that this upper storey is really an additional slice of cake. Originally the top was built of wood, and when it was burned down in AD 217 it was replaced with what we see now. This is why one has the feeling that the topmost layer does not quite fit, is itself something of an outrage in architectural terms. On this additional level we may still see a few of the metal brackets which were used to support the *velarium*, a huge canopy which protected the heads of the spectators from the sun. It is said that a special detachment of sailors was permanently quartered near the Colosseum with the main duty of tending to this vast sail awning.

Originally the Colosseum was called the Flavian amphitheatre (Rome was well served with such centres and this just happened to be the biggest), and it is probable that the name Colosseum was not used until the eighth century, by which time the spectacles had been forbidden by law. It was the Englishman, Bede, who gave us the name 'colosseum', when he called it the *colysaeus*, not in reference to the size of the building but to the nearby Colossus of Nero, which served to distinguish it from the other amphitheatres in Rome. It was this same Venerable Bede who

Aerial view of the Colosseum. Much of the marble-work of the outer storeys on this side was plundered for building purposes by medieval and Renaissance architects. The arch to the left is that of the Emperor Constantine, built in AD 312.

made the famous prophecy about the building: 'Whilst the Colosseum stands, then Rome will stand. When the Colosseum falls, then will Rome fall also, and the world with it.' In fact, the Colosseum did begin to fall, through the deprivations of man. In the Middle Ages much of the marble facing was removed, and then, during the Renaissance, whole sections of the upper part of the stone were used to build palaces and homes for the nobles. Fortunately, most of it still stands, and it is hard to imagine that anything short of an earthquake of some momentous size, or a direct hit from an atom bomb, will dislodge its incredible mass, and thus invite the end of the world.

While the Colosseum does give the impression of resting very secure upon its concrete base, the fact is that the world's third largest Roman amphitheatre – that in Verona (built in AD 290) – proved no match for an earthquake which shook northern Italy in AD 1148. Only three of the original arches to this Verona arena were left after the devastation, though the entire amphitheatre was restored in the fifteenth century, and is even

in modern times used for entertainments – though of more genteel nature than those envisaged by the Romans. However, the ruin of such a huge amphitheatre should remind us that we cannot afford to be too sanguine about the prediction made by Bede.

The human devastation of the Roman Colosseum may be seen from the side adjacent to the Arch of Constantine, marking the end of the Forum (see picture on opposite page). It is almost entirely a result of quarrying, which has removed the outer walls and galleries to leave only the inner arches beneath the tiers of seats exposed. The medieval builders who removed the marble façades and heavy stones probably felt quite justified in their work, for the Colosseum was ever associated in the popular mind with the persecutions of the Christians – the forbears of these builders. So the general feeling was that in reducing the power of such 'pagan' monuments the builders were augmenting Christianity, especially in cases where the marble 'stolen' from pagan sites was being used for church-building, and the like.

The upper tiers of arches around the Colosseum; the lower (just visible) is of the Doric order, the next one of the Ionic, the third in the Corinthian style. The topmost was a later replacement of a wooden structure, and in turn supported wooden masts which held the *velarium*, a huge protective canopy.

The Pantheon

No doubt the poet Shelley was writing in the romantic vein when he described the Pantheon as 'the visible image of the universe', for from the outside, at least, the building is not especially beautiful (unless, of course, it was precisely that which Shelley had in mind!). The Emperor Hadrian who probably designed it personally was not really a brilliant architect, and it had always been something of a problem for the Romans to bring together the idea of a professional frontage (which they were inclined to walk through, as in their triumphal arches) with a rotunda, which has by definition no clear axis.

The Roman frontage in the 'Greek manner', with its eight Corinthian columns, is pleasing enough, and no doubt it was even beautiful when the bronze statues were still in place on the pediment. The exterior of the rotunda is also quite pleasant, and here again, in former days, when still covered with its marble and stucco facing, it might have been extremely beautiful. But, the two together – the rectilinear frontage and the curvilinear rotunda – form something of an absurdity, and I find it almost impossible to stand in Piazza della Rotunda, and look towards this famous building without smiling to myself. Yet, even as I give this personal opinion, I must in fairness record that others do not always agree with me. In his fine book on Rome, Stewart Perowne records that the Pantheon is 'one of the most beautiful, most important buildings in the world'.

Once past the portico, and inside the building, the unlikely union of straight lines

Left The portico of the Pantheon, which dates from AD 124 but was reconstructed partly upon the site of an earlier temple built over a century and a half earlier.

The interior of the rotunda, looking towards the modern Christian altar.

most beautiful and perfect in design. The structure is much the same as when it was built, in spite of frequent restorations.

The rotunda is a perfect circle, with an inner diameter of 43 metres (142 feet); the vertical walls are 6 metres (20 feet) thick, with indented recesses 4 metres (14 feet) deep, each fronted with columns. The rotunda was originally covered with gilded bronze plates, which were moved by Constans II in AD 663 and taken to the 'New Rome' of Constantinople. The portico is 33 metres (110 feet) wide, and 18 metres (60 feet) deep in the centre.

The statues and decorations are gone, of course, and these must certainly have improved the feeling within. The walls were constructed to allow for eight recesses, in which stood the statues of the seven planetary gods: Apollo the Sun god, Selene as goddess of the Moon, and Mercury, Venus, Mars, Jupiter and Saturn. The eighth recess framed the onlooker, the human being who was himself by way of being an image of the gods – symbolically deified in the recess which led out into the world beyond.

The Pantheon was dedicated to all the gods, and so not surprisingly it was closed in the fourth century by the first Christian Emperors. It was saved from a threatened destruction by Pope Boniface, and then re-dedicated to Santa Maria 'ad Martyres' in reference to the fact that many of the bones of the early Christians (those who had turned their backs on 'all the gods') were transferred there from the catacombs.

The light streaming down from an 8-metre (27-foot) opening in the crown of the rotunda, from a height which is exactly the same as the diameter of the building, as the Roman theory of architectural proportion required, is quite remarkable. We are left with a feeling of technical perfection, even a certain coldness (which is the effect which perfection in art seems to have on human beings). One feels also, perhaps, that the pagan planetary gods to whom this place was originally dedicated have not yet been completely exorcized, in spite of a thousand years of Christian ritual within the building.

Art lovers may excuse this coldness when they learn that the great Raphael is buried in this ancient space, symbolically enclosed in an antique sarcophagus, lying near to the tomb of the woman he loved.

and curves is forgotten, and one stands amazed at the space within, which reveals what Shelley had in mind, for the universe itself is expressed as articulated space. Not only was this interior, constructed between AD 119 and 128, the largest enclosed space in the ancient world, but it was also one of the

The Baths of Caracalla

It has been suggested more than once that the Emperor Caracalla was quite insane by the time he opened his huge baths in Rome, in AD 217, the same year in which he was assassinated by his own praetorian guards. For at least a couple of years he had been suffering from acute delusions of grandeur (for example, believing that he was Alexander the Great, and acting accordingly), and so it has been tempting to see the very size and lavishness of these baths as a further outward sign of his madness. Over six years in the building, at a time when Romans built both quickly and well, they were reputed to be the most magnificent baths the world had ever seen. However, the symmetry of the design and the care with which each detail of the building was worked out point to anything but insanity. The truth is that records show the idea for the baths to have been drawn up by Septimius Severus, and merely completed or opened in the lifetime of Caracalla. They remained in use, a symbol of Roman luxury, for about four centuries, until the invading Goths destroyed the Marcian aqueduct which served the baths with the copious water which they needed.

The popular Roman *thermae*, as such baths were called, were indeed a sign of the taste for luxury which the pleasure-loving upper classes of the slave-served Roman society had developed, but the baths which Caracalla 'presented' with much pomp and ceremony to the Roman public were on a scale of luxury which even they considered remarkable. The ground plan of these thermae displays the Roman love of order: it is an architect's dream, beautiful even as a drawing of what might be, a symbol of the structural order which the Romans tried with such vigour and scant success to impose upon the whole world. This ground plan remains the clearest guide to what the baths must have looked like, for the ruins themselves mislead in many respects. At the centre of the building was a *natatio*, a vast swimming pool open to the sky; next to this was the most remarkable part of the construction – an enormous hall covered in high vaults carried by eight huge columns. The entire bathing area was raised on a marble platform about 6 metres (20 feet) high, underneath which were furnaces, storerooms, and the many service rooms. This platform appears to have been about 300 metres (1000 feet) long. Within, or upon, this dominant central area were various bathing rooms, which we shall look at in more detail shortly. These were surrounded by parks, with landscape gardens, fountains and statues, beyond which was an outer ring of apartments, shops and lecture rooms, as well as a series of rooms to house the large number of slaves who worked the baths.

This plan outline must have indicated that the modern word 'bath' is something of a misnomer when applied to the Roman thermae, which were something quite different from what we would nowadays expect from a bath, however complex. They were, in a sense, vast amusement arcades, or even 'civic centres', where Romans might gossip at their ease, exchange news in the days when there was virtually no other way of discovering what was going on, or merely relax before some entertainment or other.

Within the magnificent thermae of Caracalla the Romans were well served with almost every conceivable kind of relaxation and entertainment, for the complex included shopping arcades, libraries, theatres, sports stadia (where there was racing, wrestling and boxing), a picture gallery, and so on. In addition, of course, there were all the necessary facilities of the therapeutic bathing areas – a warm room (*tepidarium*), a cold room, with open baths (*frigidarium*), and a hot room (*caldarium*), which in this case was a huge hallway with a dome somewhat similar to the one still preserved in the Pantheon (see page 90). Romans could be massaged with oils,

The remains of the Baths of Caracalla in Rome are still extensive enough to give some idea of the vast size of the original.
Right Plan of the Baths as they were on completion.

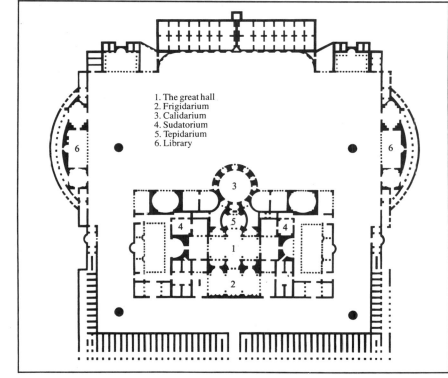

1. The great hall
2. Frigidarium
3. Calidarium
4. Sudatorium
5. Tepidarium
6. Library

and have their skin scraped, or be shampooed, in *unctuaria*, or just sweat in *sudaria*. No doubt, also, there were areas where the men might indulge their sexual propensities: historians relate that as the Empire fell into greater decadence, the thermae became the centre of increased sexual licence, and it is certain that the First Christian Emperors closed down the baths because of this.

From the poor remains which now stand in Rome it is difficult for us to picture the full former splendour of these ancient buildings. Some beautiful examples of the coloured mosaic walks, depicting athletes and bathers, can be seen in the Vatican Museum, but there are few traces now of the coloured marble fascias, or of the mosaic walls, with frescoes on stucco above. Gone are the lofty domed ceilings, splendidly painted or sheathed in glass mosaic, and the sparkling light and running water, issuing from a myriad of sculpted lions' heads and grotesques.

Leptis Magna

In his wonderfully observant and witty book, *Cities in the Sand*, the traveller Aubrey Menen recommends that those who are fortunate enough to visit the places of which he writes should save Leptis Magna to the last, for the city is 'perfect'. The word is hardly an exaggeration, for only a few of the original columns and stones of this ancient Roman city have been stolen, with the result that the sand which is being removed reveals a hidden world far more complete, and indeed perfect, than any other which has come down to us from the past. This solid piece of history lies on the coast of north-west Libya, about 65 kilometres (40 miles) from Tripoli, and bears the modern name Labdah.

Most people know that a poet, John William Burgon – who was more a biblical scholar than a poet – described the city of Petra as 'a rose red city half as old as time' (see page 48), but his imagination was perhaps too vivid, for this rock city is not rose red, whilst Leptis Magna most certainly is, and indeed, as Menen so acutely observes, when the sun is just right, it looks much like a legendary city built of gold. And if Leptis is not half as old as time, then it is at least more ancient than Petra, for it was founded by the Phoenicians in the tenth century BC.

The Phoenicians were sea traders, and so they placed their new city by an estuary, which is now long-since silted up. The harbour served the ancients well in their day, however, for it provided the Roman world across the Mediterranean with boat-loads of wild animals from Africa, for the amphitheatre entertainments. It was also, no doubt, from this same harbour that Septimius Severus set sail to become one of the really great Roman Emperors (after a few judicious murders, as was the style in those days), for this man, best known to tourists for the triumphal arch which still dominates the forum in Rome, was born in Leptis Magna.

The Romans had decided to take Leptis from the Numidians in 46 BC, for they had a keen eye on the caravan routes in the Sahara, which might be pillaged or protected as policy required. They saw also a great business potential in the wild animal trade, and injected massive capital into expansive building schemes, most of which now remain in outline against the deep blue skies.

The business scheme which led to the expansion of Leptis – the export of African animals – consciously or unconsciously influenced the Roman art which is found in such abundance there. In view of the main business of the town, it is almost a shameless confidence trick to have a most lovely pavement mosaic showing the mythical Orpheus enchanting the wild animals with his lyre. Altogether more down to earth are the frescoes in the baths at Leptis, which show gladiators in combat, with wild animals both destroying and being destroyed. It is hard for a modern mind to conceive the scale of such destruction – the fact is that the many amphitheatres were at times merely public slaughterhouses. For example, a 'celebration' organized by the Emperor Trajan to commemorate a victory over the Dacians, and which lasted for 123 days, saw the slaughter of more than 11,000 wild animals!

In Leptis they built the usual forum, which is a far more beautiful example than the famous hotchpotch in Rome, an amphitheatre – that basic necessity of Roman life – a theatre, a four-way triumphal arch, and temples, not to mention the ubiquitous Roman baths, which were built by Hadrian in AD 127. The structure of these is still preserved, and they were in their day among the largest in the Empire, though somewhat dwarfed by the later baths of Caracalla, the son of Septimius (see page 92). In such building the Romans laid the foundations for the finest remains in North Africa, if not indeed in the Western world. What set out as a fine business venture has ended up as a tribute to

Roman architecture and wealthy life-style.

Septimius Severus, though much occupied with the wars to east and west of Rome, was obviously proud of his Leptis, and continued the building programme from afar. He extended the harbour, gave it a new basilica and forum, and a monumental colonnaded street for the city which by this time had become the third largest city in Africa (next to Alexandria and Carthage), with a population of 80,000 inhabitants, mainly of Libyan-Punic stock, even though the city was officially designated a Roman colony.

The arch by which we enter the walls of Leptis was also placed there on the order of Septimius. Fallen now, its ornate grandeur would suggest that it might well have competed with the ancient baths for pride of architectural place in Leptis; yet, if design could be reduced to such competition, the palm would be awarded to the Hadrianic baths, for even slight imagination will allow one to sense the magic of those vast halls. The brightly painted stucco ceilings, the coloured marble of the high columns, and nearer the earth and water, the exquisite bright mosaics – it must have been more like an exotic palace than public baths. No wonder that the Christians closed them down – not merely because they had inevitably become the centre of 'unbridled lasciviousness', but because their very beauty must have been an affront to the asceticism of the early Christians, who in word, if not in deed, cared naught for comfort.

The basilica also introduces further thoughts about later Christianity. Yet another present from Septimius to his fair city, these were the Roman courts of law. They still stand, these courts, with high stone walls punctuated by supporting columns, inset with marble pilasters slightly more oriental than one is used to in Roman buildings, and a little reminiscent of certain French Gothic cathedrals.

Since this is one of the great Roman law buildings, in a great Roman colonial city, and the central Roman authority dispensed in the world both law and peace (modern Europe inheriting the law, but not the peace), then we might say that by standing in this particular building in Leptis Magna, we are in the hub of one of the greatest of the cogwheels which ran Rome. Yet, beyond reflections on the Roman law, an hour or so spent

in this remarkable building will show the extent to which the Roman basilica influenced the design of the Christian church and cathedral, for within this building we may see all the salient elements which were later adopted by the Christian architects. There is the columned 'nave', where the law was pleaded before judges and noisy multitudes, and to each side the 'aisles', separated from the nave by splendid columns which, by some miracle, are mainly still standing proudly in the middle of these high walls. A few have fallen, perhaps tossed there by an earthquake, and are ranged on the longitudinal axis, as though in humble prayer to a god. And there, indeed, in the direction in which they are lying, are the two massive pillars which frame the apse, and

A sculpted face of the Medusa between two arches. Much of the architectural detail in this ancient city remains perfectly preserved.

Previous page The Roman theatre at Leptis Magna, built in stone and marble. Beneath this site have been found the remains of a fifth-century BC Punic cemetery.

might well contain an altar, or some image of the Virgin Mary.

Inevitably, when the Christians did take over the deserted city, they turned this basilica into a church. There is still a marble pulpit, somewhat reminiscent of pulpits one might find in much later churches in southern Italy. It is significant that a pulpit had only to be rigged together from some broken stones to transform this Roman law building into a place for Christian worship. There is a great lesson and moral in these few stones raised within the vast and ruined splendour of the Septimius Basilica!

One of the most delightful things about this city is its state of preservation. Archaeologists have not yet carried off the stiff-bodied statues to their museums. Therefore we have a rare opportunity to see such sculptures as the Dioscuros in the theatre, perhaps standing in the very place for which he was intended – a remarkable thing for any ancient statue, two thousand years later – even if this particular figure was very probably imported from Rome. Or again, one may see the very

Roman youth, pretending to be a Greek (an occupation favoured by many statues in those days) among the colonnaded walks of the baths of Hadrian, the white of his marble flesh contrasting most beautifully with the warm golds of the building.

One may almost enjoy still the atmosphere of the market place, adorned as it is with over a hundred columns, protected from the sun and the rare inclemencies, in a colonnade which runs around the market place, as though to cloister it off from the outer peace of the world, in a curious inversion of the idea of the Christian religious cloisters.

Among the most interesting survivals, so well preserved that one could almost use them today, are the standard measures, designed and displayed to ensure fair trading in the market itself. Set in the wall is a block incised with linear measures, and with squares, to regulate the sale of cloths, yarns and so on. In huge stone plinths, resting on animal feet, a series of volumetric depressions are let into the surface to act as standards for the sale of liquids and the like.

Leptis is not only well preserved, but it is also not so spoiled by tourism as other ancient sites. To stand in or near the bowl of the theatre, and to look out across its crescent towards the dense forest of tall columns, many of them still bearing the architraves on their Corinthian capitals, is to experience the sense that one is standing in a ghost city, that time has somehow looped back on itself. In few other places is there the same sense of the pressure of the past, the same feeling that one may catch a glimpse from the corner of an eye of a ghost of some Roman colonial. And yet, this sense of preservation, so unlike any other sites, should not lead one to think that the city has not had an uneventful history since the Roman Empire collapsed, and the Romans so abruptly left the African coasts. The history of the city is almost the history of Europe: the Vandals put certain finishing touches to a steady deterioration of the city after the third century, and from about AD 455 the walls remained buried in the sands until the Christian Byzantines arrived and put together their pulpit, and added this time not more temples, but churches. Then this house of Christian dreams was knocked down by the Arabs in the great invasion which threatened the whole of Europe, and almost engulfed the Mediterranean itself.

General view of the colonnaded market place.

INDIA

Small but intricately beautiful Muktesvar temple
at Bhuvanesvar.

Bhuvanesvar

Among the wonders of India must be included the holy city of Bhuvanesvar, located on the swampy coast of Orissa, some 20 kilometres (12 miles) south of the Mahanadi delta. This city of temples is sometimes called 'the Cathedral City of India', more in the spirit of describing the grandeur of its temples, than of equating their use to that of Christian churches.

An inscription on a rock, a few kilometres to the south of the city, records the conquest of the area by King Asoka in the third century. The campaign was so bloody that it opened his eyes to the horrors of war, and he decided to settle peacefully in the area with no thought of further expansion. Later the site was occupied by the Shailodbhava dynasty, who built a large number of temples, followed by the Gangas, and later still by Muslim invaders. This potted history indicates something of the complexity of the archaeology underlying these sites, which represents a panorama of Orissan art from the third century BC to the late sixteenth century.

The most important of the early temple buildings was put in hand during the seventh century, when tradition records that 'several thousand' temples were built. Of these only thirty of any real size or architectural significance remain. These were built around or near the Bindu Sagar lake, which is said to contain water brought from every sacred stream and reservoir in India. Each year an idol from the nearby Lingaraja temple is brought to this lake for ritual immersion.

The temples are various in style, but all have a strange, organic quality, as if they have sprung up out of the earth. They have a similar basic pattern in which the curvilinear structure of the *sikhara,* crowned by an *amalaka,* rests on a shrine, the *garbhagrha,* which holds at least one sculpted image of a god. Sometimes there is a porch hallway (the *natmandir*) in front. All the temples, for all their complex appearance, are actually very simple in construction, being built almost entirely of corbelled vaulting, in a series of what might be described as hollow pyramids, piled on top of one another.

The temples may be divided into two basic types according to design. There is the *rekha,* which is a conical, beehive form with a spire, and the *bhadra,* which is a kind of terraced pyramid. Since a few of the early written architectural guides have survived from the times when these temples were constructed, it is possible to form some idea of the intentions of the designers. We know, for example, that the rekha was intended to be a material image of the cosmic man, and the names given to the different parts of the building correspond to parts of the human body – there is a trunk, a neck, a head, and so on. We also know that the sikharas, the stone mounds with spires, are intended to be symbols of the mythical Mount Meru, the ancient home of the gods.

The worship for which these temples were built was connected with the sexual nature of man, especially with the destructive and creative power of the *linga,* or phallus, which is associated with the cult of the god Siva.

This Siva was the 'Destroyer' of the creative work of Brahma – the old had to be destroyed to make way for the created new. The destructive agent was the special fire which was said to emanate from his 'third eye', which is a *chakra,* or 'wheel of power', which exists in the space between the ordinary eyes. This powerful energy was said to have been created out of the darkness which resulted when his wife Parvati covered his eyes with her hands. Siva also destroyed through the use of a bolt from his trident, which is symbolized on top of some of the temples in Bhuvanesvar.

The recipient of the force from this linga is the feminine *yoni,* the passive sexual parts of the female goddess with whom Siva dances

throughout Hindu art in rhythms of extraordinary intensity.

It is the connection of this potent destructive force with what is both its opposite and complementary, the power of erotic energy, that accounts for the feature of the temples that most strikes European visitors, the sculptures of copulating couples, known as *mithuna*. While the interiors of the temples are usually almost stark in their simplicity, except for the image of the god itself, the outsides are incredibly complex, being completely covered with relief carving. These carvings, from sources both sacred and profane, include depictions in great detail of the 'amorous postures' of the mithuna. Altogether they constitute an entire world spectrum in stone, depicting every level of being both known and unknown, stretching from the dark level of the demons to the upper world of the Devic kingdom, and incorporating the human levels which stand between. The idea is for all of life to be reflected upon the surface of the temple. As the Indian poet Rabindranath Tagore said when writing of Bhuvanesvar, 'The abode of God has been enveloped by a variety of figures depicting the good and the evil, the great as well as the insignificant, the daily occurrences of human life . . . This life is His Eternal Temple.' The message of such statue-filled walls is indeed that God is everywhere, in everything, in the silence and in the midst of life and death, even in the heart of separation and the union of the mithuna.

The oldest of the temples in Bhuvanesvar is the Parashurameshwar, the porch of which is well known for its stone lattice windows and wonderful dancing dwarfs. A couple of hundred metres to the east of this magnificent building stands the small Muktesvar, which has been called 'a dream realized in sandstone', its surface undulating with figures of men and of gods, and of the amorous mithuna couples. Behind this is the Kedaresvar temple, with a ground plan which is almost circular, containing a 2·4 metre (8-foot) statue of the Monkey god Hanuman alongside the figure of the goddess Durga standing triumphant on a lion.

The most famous of the temples is no doubt the Lingaraja, which was built about AD 1000, the main tower of which is over 54 metres (180 feet) high. It is more complex in its ground plan than most of the other temples, with an axial grouping of halls for religious rites and dancing and one or two small pilgrim rooms. The temple and its outbuildings are actually marked off by a compound wall, 156 by 140 metres (520 by 465 feet); entrance to these walls is forbidden to all but Hindus, but a ramp has been constructed nearby which permits the non-Hindu visitor a reasonable view of the religious precinct as a whole. The tower wall, which is about 2 metres (7 feet) thick, has inset an interior staircase by means of which the faithful may climb to the top. The outside of the temple is lavishly decorated with the usual pantheon of gods and spiritual beings, as well as the ubiquitous mithuna couples.

By extensive study of the designs and decorative elements of the thirty surviving ancient temples, historians have divided the site into four different areas of development.

The first period, from the seventh to the ninth century, gave rise to a number of fairly modestly sized temples with curvilinear sikharas, the walls of which are divided into

Detail of the decorative sculpture which covers the Muktesvar temple.

102

three vertical segments, the middle one being more decorative than the others. The oldest representative temples of this period are the Satrughneshwar and the Parashurameshwar, followed by the Markandeshwar temple and the Shishireshwar. These temples are situated around the Bindu Sagar lake, and it is quite likely from their style that they were built under the influence of architects from other parts of India. Despite the decorations on the outsides, their interiors are noticeably austere.

The second period, from the late ninth to the tenth century, comprises temples with five main vertical bands on the sikharas, and with more complex supporting halls – in some cases built in the form of terraced pyramids. The division of the walls into a greater number of units means that the decorative sculptures are smaller and more detailed. Figures appear on the brackets which separate the niches holding the larger carvings. The most lovely example of the temples built during this period is the Muktesvar, which is amongst the most beautiful Indian temples, and is indeed regarded by some as the very finest of all.

The third period, which includes the eleventh and twelfth centuries, is represented by a large number of temples, each reaching skywards with a greater dignity than those of the previous periods. The sikharas give the impression of being loftier, and, while still fivefold in their vertical structure, of being richer in decoration, as well as being surrounded by a number of towers gathered around the main halls of the temple. These temple styles are best seen in the Lingaraja and the Rajarani, the former being said by many connoisseurs to be the finest in Orissan art.

With the fourth period, which ends in the fifteenth century, there are increases in the number of vertical divisions of the sikharas, as well as an even greater abundance of surface decoration. However, there is a strong tendency in the temples built at this time towards too much decorative sculpture on the exterior, so that the external walls appear to be weighed down. Also, much of the decoration lacks the freshness and originality of the earlier work, although there are some striking exceptions. The temples of the final period include the Megheshwar and the Parvati.

Altogether, the temples and shrines in this remarkable city were said to number thousands at one time. Now only thirty major temples remain, and, of the 7000 magnificent tombs, only some 500 are in existence today, but Bhuvanesvar still stands as one of the glories of Hindu architecture.

Detail of high relief sculpture of a temple dancer, from the external decoration of the Muktesvar temple.

Sanchi

The Great Stupa at Sanchi.

The great King Asoka, that historical figure intimately involved with the spread of Buddhism, is said to have distributed almost all the remains of Buddha (save those he could not reach since they were guarded by the snake spirits, the *nagas*) to some 84,000 *stupas*, or monumental burial tombs, throughout the land of India. The great stupa in Sanchi (which is now a small village in Central Madhya Pradesh, the ancient name of which was Kakanada) is the remains of one of these burial tombs, one of the eight which Asoka had built there in the third century BC.

The survival of even this stupa is due almost entirely to accident. With the decline of Buddhism in India, the vast religious centre of ancient Kakanada was literally forgotten, and because the place was 'lost' and overgrown with vegetation, it escaped the devastations of Aurangzeb, who swept through India in the seventeenth century, destroying everything in his path. The stupas and other remains were therefore untouched until the amateur archaeologists of the nineteenth century looted and damaged them. Even so, the remains of what must have been an enormous centre may be traced back to a rich period of Buddhism, stretching from the third century BC up to the twelfth century AD – a period of uninterrupted culture rare in the history of the world.

The hill upon which the remains of Sanchi are found is perhaps the ancient Cetyyagiri, 'the mount of the sanctuary', mentioned in the very earliest Buddhist scripts. Certainly, the stupa dates from such times, for even its hemispherical shape points to the archaic design of the early stupas. It was believed that the original stupas were simple earthen burial mounds, with the result that the earliest ones, such as this main one in Sanchi, resemble essentially a mound of earth, faced with stones. Whilst the original Sanchi stupa was built entirely of stone, it took its present dimensions from a later casing of stone added in the Shunga period: it is 32 metres (106 feet) in diameter, and 13 metres (42 feet) high. Almost certainly this stonework would have been covered with stucco, and painted. Around the stupa there is a terrace designed for ritual walks, in which pilgrims follow a huge circle a prescribed number of times:

three, seven, fourteen or even 108 circuits! On the ground level is yet another such walk, protected by one of the Indian 'antique' railings – an imitation in stone of a wooden fence.

The four gateways, or *torana*, are the real glory of Sanchi. These are orientated slightly off course from the true cardinal points, the explanation for this being that such deviations confuse evil spirits. The gates are covered in the most exquisite carving, in what is now called the 'Sanchi style', which developed in the century between 50 BC and AD 50 – although, as with all things Indian, the style represents the perfection of something already well established and ancient. The sur-

face is covered with a complex undulation of sculpted details, stories and symbols overlapping and interweaving in a most complex manner: here we see elephants, horses, peacocks, lotus scrollworks, the monster *makaras* (which are associated with the Capricorn Goat-fish of the European zodiac), winged lions, ordinary people and spiritual beings. As is consistent with the practice of early Buddhist art, the physical body of the final incarnation of Buddha is not itself presented, but is merely symbolized. For example, in the sections which present what are known as the 'four great miracles' – which are really the four great historic moments in the life of Buddha – the birth of the child is expressed in the lotus, his great enlightenment is symbolized by an image of the bodhi tree (casting its shadow over the throne); the Buddha's first sermon is represented in the raised wheel of the law (the *chakra*), whilst the fourth of the 'miracles', the *paranirvana*, which is usually mistranslated in the West as 'total extinction' (which is almost the opposite of what the word means) is symbolized by the stupa, which represents death, the entry into the spiritual world.

Each of the four gateway toranas tells a multitude of stories, but within the tales are secret parables in stone, which are even more worthy of attention. The western gateway, besides giving images of the previous incarnations of the Buddha, and various stories from his final incarnation, tells a story relating to a (symbolic) previous life which points to one of the laws of destiny (*karma*), which is said to express itself in every human life in so far as certain actions are done as compensation or adjustment for previous actions. Here we see Buddha before he attained the state of Buddhahood, living as a six-tusked elephant with two elephant wives. He was more attached to one of these wives, and this naturally upset the other one. When in the next life the three were brought together once more, the rejected wife was a powerful queen, and organized great elephant hunts in order to kill off elephants. Here we see symbolized the idea that a wish or desire must always find a fulfilment on the physical plane, even if life-times intervene between the growth of the wish and its final expression. This is one of the ideas embodied in Buddhism, and beautifully symbolized on this western torana.

The southern gateway, which is the oldest of the toranas, shows as one of the most important of its pictures the birth of Buddha, with his mother Maya on a lotus surrounded by elephants, while on other parts of the gateway we see incidents from the *Jataka* tales which relate to episodes from the various lives of the Buddha in his previous incarnations.

The eastern gateway shows scenes from the life of Buddha at the time when he decided to leave his comfortable palace life in search of spiritual truth. The fact that the confines of Buddhist art demanded that his physical body should not be portrayed has led in this torana to interesting pictorial devices: for example, the footprints of Buddha are used to show the stages of his journeys, and a riderless horse to show when he travels on horse-back. This gateway shows the strange dream of Maya, the mother of the future Buddha, in which she sees an elephant standing on the moon, symbol of the child she has just conceived.

The northern gateway is by far the best preserved of this stupa, and was originally surmounted by a Buddhist 'wheel of law'. Among the rich carvings we may see a throne, symbol of the invisible Buddha, to which honey is being offered by a monkey, as well as a miracle in which the Buddha walked on air.

Of the eight stupas which King Asoka was supposed to have built at Sanchi, only three remain. One to the north-east of the main building was badly damaged by the nineteenth-century excavations, during which time Cunningham disturbed and removed the remains of the two great disciples of Buddha, Sariputra and Mahamogalana, and in 1853 sent them to London. Eventually the remains were returned to India, and are now lodged in a *vihara* (monastery) in Sanchi. Like the main stupa, this also has a ritual walk.

Another notable monument in Sanchi is the Gupta Temple, with its flat roof, and a curiously Grecian portico. Such early buildings (perhaps originally of the fourth century) are of considerable architectural interest for their central element is the *garbha*, a cubical shrine, which was to form the innermost sanctum of the later buildings, as for example in the magnificent *sikhara* temples of such sites as Khajuraho (see page 112).

The ornate north gateway, or *torana*, of the stupa at Sanchi.

107

The Ajanta Caves

In the India of 1819, shortly after the war with Nepal, a party of British army officers, out hunting in the Indhyadri hills (about 110 kilometres (70 miles) north-east of Aurangabad), accidentally discovered a series of well-hidden caves. These proved to be man-made, and were later called the Ajanta caves, after the Anglo-Indian form of the nearest village of Ajuntha.

The caves had been cut into the horseshoe curves of a wild gorge overlooking the Waghora, a river dangerous and spectacular with its high waterfalls in the rainy season, but a drab trickle in the dry season. If the scene was splendid and romantic on the outside of the cliff, in both natural forms and in the architectural frontage carved on the volcanic rock face, it was quite sublime on the inside, for the caves proved to contain sculptures and paintings of a quite rare and compelling beauty.

Further studies of the caves showed that they had been cut into the rock by two quite different Buddhist communities, who had used primitive tools, such as pick-axes, requiring an almost unbelievable expense of human labour. The first group had worked and lived there from about the second century BC, whilst the second group, Mahayana Buddhists, had moved in after the caves had been deserted for some time, and had stayed there until the seventh or eighth century AD. This latter group extended the earlier caves, and produced murals which have been described by experts as being among the finest in all India.

The caves are now easy to reach, but when they were discovered, the steps leading up to them, cut into the rock, had been eroded. Now new steps have been built to make the caves accessible to tourists. Four of the caves are *caitya*s (sanctuaries, where the community might meet), whilst twenty-five are *vihara*s (monasteries), which house the finest of the murals.

The caves are now given numbers to help distinguish them, in an order running from west to east; these numbers bear no relation to their order of construction or date. Cave no. 10 is probably the oldest, dating from the second century BC. It is a caitya, about 30 metres (100 feet) long, about 12 metres (40 feet) wide, and 13 metres (43 feet) high: the interior is supported by octagonal pillars which are cut into the living rock, leaving two aisles which run up to and behind the *stupa* or shrine.

The subjects of the murals relate either to stories from the life of the Buddha, or to themes derived from the account of his previous lives on earth, the Jataka tales, at least twelve different stories from which are found on the walls.

These stories are in many cases much older than Buddhism, but they were adopted and retold in order to point morals relating to the hidden messages connected with the doctrine of 'rebirth' and 'karma' which is central to Buddhism. It is karma which is said to determine the special pattern of a lifetime, and to condition the various opportunities, encounters with others, and obstacles which appear in each incarnation, and which are said to be a consequence of previous lifetimes and actions. One of the duties of a Buddhist is to lead his life in such a way as to face responsibly the consequences of accumulated debts from the past, and to strive as fully as possible to build only beneficial karma for future lifetimes – his aim being eventually to free himself from the 'wheel of rebirth' which ties him to ordinary consciousness in life.

In the 'life of Buddha' series of murals we see the visit of Asita to the new-born child, the temptation of Mara, legends of the Naga, or serpent race, battle scenes, the carrying of the holy relics to Ceylon, and so on. In the many details of the forest scenery in which the main actions of the paintings are set, we see the familiar and supernatural world combined. Monkeys and birds of our familiar world are depicted alongside such curious beings as the *guyaksa*, superhumans who guard treasure, and live in mountain caves, something like the European gnomes. There are the hairy pygmies, called *kirata*, who have private parts so long that they dangle to their ankles, and horse-headed *kinnara*, the tailed musicians of the mountain gods. Among

such mythical and religious subjects we may perhaps be surprised to find a fresco which shows the reception at an Indian Palace of a Persian embassy, painted in the seventh century AD.

One important mural tells the story of the final incarnation of Buddha, in which his mother, Queen Maya, the wife of Raja Suddhodana, dreams that a white elephant with six tusks has entered her body through her right side (the later birth appears also to be 'virginal'). This dream is interpreted by the Brahmans as a sign that the child to be born will be either a mighty king in the material world, or, should he choose to renounce that destiny of kingship, a great Buddha. Maya dies seven days after giving birth, in accordance with the tradition that held that no mother would be able to bear watching her child renounce the ordinary way of life.

Another cave, listed as no. 17, is said by some experts to be the finest so far as pictorial quality is concerned, though the subject matter might well have disturbed the ladies of

Mural from cave 17 at Ajanta. The cave has some of the finest of the paintings at the site.

Previous page
The cliff façade of the Ajanta Caves, now made more accessible by the building of new roads in modern times.

the British Raj. In one mural a prince is shown making love to a princess, whilst Buddha tames a wild elephant (perhaps in a symbolism related to the sexual act, which Buddha himself renounced as a hindrance to obtaining enlightenment).

One mural in the series has become quite famous, though it is generally misunderstood. This is the picture of the so-called 'dying princess' who is in fact no dying female, but the wife of Prince Nanda, the Buddha's half-brother, swooning at the news that her husband has decided to leave her and his court, in order to devote himself to the religious life. One art historian has described this image in rapturous terms: 'For pathos and sentiment and the unmistakable way of telling its story, this picture, I consider, cannot be surpassed in the history of art. The Florentines could have put better drawing, and the Venetians better colour, but neither could have thrown greater expression into it.'

An extraordinary series in cave no. 17 shows the seven Buddhas of the past, and the *Maitreya* Buddha, who is to come in the future of the present world. These same walls also depict beautiful dancing girls, and the outstanding 'wheel of life' which shows the twelve Nidanas, the causes of rebirth. This relates to one of the most abstruse of oriental doctrines, the understanding of which is said to solve the riddle of life, and to prepare the mind for the ultimate attainment of eternal bliss (*nirvana*).

These lovely paintings are usually called frescoes in the guide books (and even in scholarly works) but in fact they are mural paintings done in the tempera technique. They are painted on to a specially prepared wall surface, made smooth with an initial coating of plaster, clay, cowdung and rice-husks, on top of which was smoothed a fine hard plaster. The actual painting was done on to this dried surface, the colour being bound to its smooth plaster finish with a coating of egg-yolk. Recent scientific tests have shown that, with the exception of the costly blue of the ultramarine (made from the semi-precious stone lapis lazuli), all the colours were of local mineral origin and were collected on or near the site.

In the Indian literature of the seventh century there appears only one known reference to these caves, given in the personal records of a pilgrim. 'In the east of this country was a mountain range, ridges one above another in succession, tiers of peaks and sheer summits. Here was a monastery, the base of which was in a dark defile, and its lofty walls were quarried in the cliff and rested on the peak . . . This monastery was built by Achala of Western India.' The pilgrim then describes one of the sanctuaries which (save for a little exaggeration) corresponds to one of the caves, 'a large temple above 100 feet high, in which was a stone image of the Buddha above 70 feet high – the image was surmounted by a tier of seven canopies unattached and unsupported, each separated from the one above it by the space of 3 feet'. From such a level description of what actually does exist in this curious part of the world, the pilgrim then breaks into traveller's fantasy, for he tells how 'outside the gate of this monastery, on either side, north and south, was a stone elephant . . . and the bellowing of these elephants caused earthquakes'.

The interior of the nave-like cave 26. The stupa at the far end has been carved out of the rock.

Khajuraho

The town of Khajuraho in northern India, where once there stood a complex of eighty-five large temples, of which twenty splendid examples still survive, conjures in the popular mind not images of temples, but erotic sculptures of lovers, the *mithuna* of the ancient Indian pantheon. Even the popular guide books, restrained in their prose, have to admit the prurience of these statues of couples making love in every imaginable posture and position, if only to avoid offending visitors. They advise the gentle tourist that the statues are 'too revealing for the excessively sensitive'.

Yet, of course, the mithuna couples are only a small part of these incredible temples which were raised by the Candella kings, a thousand years and more ago. These couples are merely the decorative elements reflective of a profound tantric philosophy which sees sexual activity as the manifestation of a struggle between destructive and creative cosmic powers. They are therefore quite appropriate as surface ornamentation on these masses of soaring masonry.

The buildings dazzle with the profusion of the sculptures and with the thick encrustations of ornament. Gods and goddesses, celestial beings, nymphs, handmaidens and human beings jostle with serpents and demons and the provocative mithunas. This is the art of architecture taken to its extreme – a beautifully conceived mass rendered as an undulating surface of decoration. Each of the twenty remaining temples has a distinctive style, but they all belong to a strain of temple design which is quite unique in that period – though it appears to have influenced greatly the development of later Indian forms.

The spires of Khajuraho are more dome-like than most other Indian temples, and there is an impression of squatness because the *sikhara* are surrounded below by numerous small turrets (*urusringa*), which lend to the entire temple the appearance of a dominant mountain peak, set in a rich outcropping of smaller mountains and high foothills. Since each of the many turrets, as well as the main tower itself, is lavishly decorated, the general effect is one of great magnificence, the unity of sculptural effect within the rich texture being the predominant quality. It is not at all surprising that the historians should point to the Gothic cathedrals of Europe as the equivalents of these pagan temples. There exists in their forms the same sense of spiritual aspiration, the same remarkable feeling for the balance between mass and decorative texture, and the same unity of conception, which leaves the onlooker with the feeling that not one detail could be changed without detriment to the whole.

The finest example of this Khajuraho style is the *Kandarya Mahadeva*, which was built around AD 1000. It was dedicated to Siva, and contains a statue of him with the trident symbol, his hair in its conical coiffure (intended to represent the Ganges river), with at his feet the bull of Nandi. This is the most richly decorated of the Khajuraho temples, and one meticulous observer has counted 872 statues inside and outside the temple. It is raised upon a high terrace of stonework, approached by means of a monumental stairway. The shrine itself is high in the walls of the temple, and is entered by way of steps which continue the stairway from ground level. The presence of this rounded entrance so high above the actual foundations of the terrace-borne series of friezes, columns and urus-ringas lends an organic feeling to the temple, as though it were the home of some vast animal, rather than a place of pagan worship.

This temple, while very representative in its style and details of the architecture special to Khajuraho, is still an expression of the predominant architectural philosophy of India, for like the other temples and stupas, its form reflects a hidden symbolism. One of the main intentions behind the form is to relate it to the mythical mountain of Meru (see also page 126). The mithunas who interweave upon the surface of the 'sacred mount' which is the temple are associated with the ideal of unity which is supposed to be found in this mythical home of the spirit. The male and the female are expressions of a polarity which occurred only when the spiritual world first descended into matter, and then withdrew. The sexual impulse is seen as the outward sign of the wish to establish once more the sense of union which existed before that time, and which indeed still exists in Mount Meru. Thus, far from being the salacious illustrations of a depraved paganism, the mithunas are indeed the outer form of a highly sophisticated philosophy, pointing to an explanation of the urges in all human beings.

In view of this it is hardly surprising that the two most important gods of the pantheon to whom these temples are dedicated are related to aspects of human sexuality – these being Siva and Visnu. The cult image of the three-headed, eight-armed Siva, which is one of the most famous of the non-sexual images from this city, is in the temple of Jagdamba, dedicated to Visnu, Parvati and Kali.

The oldest of the Khajuraho temples is the one dedicated to Kali. This is the Chaunsath, the Indian name being related to the number sixty-four, which is the total of female servants who were dedicated to the service of the Hindu god, and who served within this temple from about AD 900. Each of these women had a small cell within the sacred precinct, of which some thirty-five still remain reasonably intact.

Some historians, however, rate the Lakshmana as the masterpiece of this religious centre. Its elephant friezes are famous, but it is as usual the erotic scenes which take pride of place. These include *bandham*, the 'intertwining' intercourse, with both figures standing, each with a raised leg twisted around the waist of the other. Perhaps less aesthetic, we find here also examples of oral sex, bestiality, and a wide variety of different sexual combinations.

For a full appreciation of this type of art, we need to translate ourselves into the way of thinking which obviously permeated the outlook of the Indians of the tenth century, and see sex as a striving towards spiritual union. If we can see the sexual act in its aspiration, rather than in its mere physical activity, then we may be able to view the mithuna couples, which decorate the sides of these 'mountains of Meru', in a new way. That a new approach is demanded of the modern mind is evident from the traditional Indian interpretation of the curious sculpture known as the *antavala*, which is found on the walls of the Kandarya Mahadeva. This shows Siva having intercourse with one female, whilst manipulating

The magnificent
Visvanatha temple.

the bodies of two others, in preparation for further copulation. This view of sex occasions a curious twist of logic, as Siva's act is generally interpreted as a great sacrifice on his part!

In Europe and America we have been conditioned to think of sex mainly from the point of view of its physical aspects in terms of personal gratification or in relation to the begetting of children. While these are, of course, important elements in human life they are certainly not the elements which these mithuna are intended to comment upon. The statuary is almost certainly concerned with what we might call the 'cosmological' aspect of sex, that is, with the transformation of human sexual energies into a higher plane. The assumption (or perhaps we should say the sure knowledge, for that is what it was to the Hindu sculptors) underlying this is that, just as ordinary untransformed sexual energies may give rise to the birth of children, so may sexual energies which have been transformed by meditation or by special spiritual disciplines give birth to the 'inner child' which lies within every human being.

Siva, one of the most important figures in the Hindu pantheon, is indeed concerned with sexuality, as stated above. He is often seen as a destructive figure and is popularly known as the Destroyer (see page 100), with reference to the potential for violence in the sexual forces. There is, however, another side to his character, embodied in his function as a redeemer inclined to use what is degenerate or decaying for a higher or a spiritual purpose.

The view that sexual energy may redeem and can be applied to higher spiritual ends is, of course, not unique to the Hindu religion – nor, indeed, are the mithuna figures unique for they find a distinct echo in copulating humans (King and Queen, Sun and Moon) in European alchemical symbolism – and such ideas are expressed, although somewhat less sensually, in the symbolism of the Church. For example, the snake, and sometimes the scorpion, is a symbol of the lower sexual energies, while the eagle is the symbol of these same energies after they have been refined by spiritual exercises. This explains why the zodiacal sign of Scorpio, which has also been linked with Siva, is given two symbols, the scorpion and the eagle, of which one is bound to earth while the other may fly off into the spiritual world. Probably, the widely misunderstood ideal of chastity, as practised in most monastic establishments, was derived from the wish to redeem the sexual energies and to give birth to the inner man, rather than from the notion that there was something essentially 'wrong' with the sexual act itself.

One feels that it is only such a view as this, permitting of a higher level of sexuality, which may intelligently explain the presence of the exotic and salacious figures on the walls of buildings intended for religious purposes. If one looks closely at the faces of these god-like figures one does not see stamped on them the grimace of human passion, of the lower human nature, presented in an act of sensual limitation; one sees instead a grace of spirit and a profundity of calm, which might express the fact that the figures are involved not in selfish gratification but in a conscious sacrifice to the spiritual beings and gods. Here one finds no expression of that human involvement which Shakespeare described as 'an expense of spirit in a waste of shame' – one sees spirit rising triumphant. This ability to transform evil forces, or difficult external circumstances, is recounted in the story of how the gathered evil forces of the world attempted to subdue him. First together they fashioned a huge serpent to crush him, but the god twisted it around his neck and its coils were turned into a necklace. Then they sent a tiger to devour him but he draped it over his shoulders, and it became a mantle to protect him. Finally the evil forces sent a more human figure in the shape of a hideous dwarf with a twisted spine; but Siva stepped on the humanoid's neck, broke its spine, and crushed it, so that its body became a platform for Siva's eternal dance.

High-relief sculpture, depicting a group of musicians, from the Lakshmana temple.

CEYLON AND SOUTH- EAST ASIA

View from the top of the third level of the stupa
at Borobudur, Java.

Anuradhapura

According to legend, the daughter of the King of Bengal seduced a savage lion, and from the union was born a boy named Sihabahu, who eventually ascended to the throne. He in turn fathered a son, Vijaya, who appeared to have inherited the lion strain, for his violence led to his being exiled from India and becoming king of nearby Ceylon.

Lion-man or not, the fierce Vijaya is an historical figure, and round about 500 BC he did invade Ceylon and take up kingship there by force of arms, subduing the native *yaksa*, the so-called 'devil worshippers', in the process. His leonine energies appear to have been translated into a creative force more appropriate to kingship, and a huge and prosperous civilization ensued. Later, in the third century, the island of Ceylon – the 'land without sorrows' – was permeated with the spirit of Buddhism, and to so great an extent that the relics of Buddha were brought there for safekeeping. From this Buddhism grew well-rooted in Ceylon, more so than in its native home of India.

The city Anuradhapura, which was to become the capital of Ceylon for almost a millennium and a half, with a name which means 'city of happy people', grew in these early years. Despite the major breaks in continuity of the religion, as for example when Ceylon was taken by Elara, and the usual periodic plunder and rapine associated with the growth of any civilization, the city prospered.

One of the earliest non-Sinhalese accounts of the magnificent city of Anuradhapura is that given by a Chinese pilgrim, Fa Hian. He writes in the most glowing terms of his period of study there in AD 412, describing the grandeur of the buildings, the splendour of the numerous processions, and the general culture of the people. In particular he admired the university where he was allowed to study, for here the subjects of law, medicine, astrology, literature and irrigation were among the main areas of research. It was here also that the words of the sacred Pali writings were committed to memory, handed down in an oral tradition, in sounds which were no longer really understood.

The buildings must certainly have been impressive. The almost legendary, yet quite historical King Dutthagamani, had, in the first century BC, built the *Lohapasada*, the 'Brazen Palace', so called because it was covered in bronze tiles. This was an enormous pyramidal structure resting upon a square platform supported by a thousand granite pillars (still standing to this day), each side of which was 45 metres (150 feet) long, and towering to the same height. It had nine storeys, each said to contain a hundred rooms, with silver furnishings, and gems, festooned with gold. 'In this palace', the *Mahawamsa*, the 'Great Chronicle' of Sinhalese Buddhism, poetically records, 'there were a thousand dormitories having windows with ornaments which were as bright as eyes.' The central hall was supported on golden pillars in the form of lions and supernatural beings, and in the centre of this hall, which held the seven treasures, there was an enchanting throne, adorned with a golden sun, a silver moon, and pearl stars.

The city also contained the famous 'Gold-dust' *dagaba*, built also by Dutthagamani to hold the sacred footprint of Buddha, along with other important relics. This was built of brick, and was over 81 metres (270 feet) high, and 88 metres (294 feet) in diameter. One European who visited it described it as something like 'a colossal red balloon, crowned with a dazzling white and golden top'. Finally, the city held the Ruanwelli-saye, built by the same king, standing in the centre of a huge granite square, with sides some 150 metres (500 feet) in length, all sculptured in elephantine forms, supporting the superstructure upon it. Altogether nine such

The *Jetawanarama dagaba* at Anuradhapura, in Sri Lanka (Ceylon).

colossal public buildings were listed in the records, yet in a sense these were dwarfed by the vast irrigation enterprises which were undertaken to provide the city with copious water supplies.

An enormous reservoir was constructed in AD 450, some eighty kilometres (fifty miles) from the city, much of which may be seen today. This 'black lake', as it was called, had a circumference of eighty kilometres, and a complex system of canals and irrigation channels to carry the water both to the city and outlying areas. This city reservoir was

said to have been the most stupendous irrigation system in the world.

Water works, intended for pleasure, for religious purposes or for pure agriculture, appear to have been one of the specialities of the early Sinhalese architects. The exquisite *kuttam pokuna*, the 'twin baths', which are surrounded by flights of steps and decorative elements, along with the pleasure garden pools of *Ran Masu*, built in the eighth century, are still preserved, still surprising in the tranquillity of their ancient design. In this latter system of bathing pools, much use of natural formations has been harmoniously united into the design – for example, well-chosen boulders and stones are incorporated into the cascades and rivulets of waterfalls, whilst in contrast such 'natural forms' as elephants are cut immobile in the stone, themselves appearing to bathe within the waters. A pool is cut into the body of a huge rock and built up outwards from hand-carved stones, shored up with sculpted stonework. These original formations have invited a natural comparison with the fountains of Bernini in Rome, but a more evocative and accurate comparison might be made with the houses and settings of the modern architect Frank Lloyd Wright.

The city's huge buildings were covered in minute architectural details, and in paintings and sculptured forms which decorated them inside and out. Of these, sculptures of the sensuous and delicate rotund female forms of early Sinhalese art have become famous. The prurience of the body is touched off by provocative nuances of jewellery – yet these women belong to the spiritual world, to the ideal of womanhood, rather than to the realm of the merely sensuous, sexual or fantastical. They are great works of art, whose true meaning rests in invisible realms, rather than in the physical: they point to strengths in women, rather than to weaknesses in man. Nothing quite like these works has ever been produced in European art, and we, so used to the weakness of the flesh permeating our view of art, rarely approach such sculptures in the right frame of mind.

Surrounded by this amazing opulence of external form, a simple bodhi tree grew, the Buddhist tree of wisdom. It had been planted there by King Tissa, who had taken it from a

The 'Gold-dust' dagaba (*right*), built by King Dutthaganimi. The immensity of this brick building may be gauged by comparison with the fair-sized stupa which appears to the left of it, which is the same size as the one below from elsewhere on the site.

was intimately connected with the introduction and spread of Buddhism in Ceylon; it was here that the son of the great Asoka preached in the third century, and the centre is regarded as the very cradle of Sinhalese Buddhism. One of the most famous of the architectural points in the monastery is the 'snake' bathing pool, the *naga pokuna*, a cistern some 40 metres (130 feet) long cut from the living rock, with an enormous rock cobra poising its head over the top.

Descriptions of the city amaze, and so easily degenerate into a mere juggling with colossal figures which run through the mind and leave the imagination stunned. The archaeologist Cottrell gives figures for other cities – expresses in numerals the might of Babylon, the weight of Egypt, for example – yet those given for this city of Anuradhapura somehow shame the others to silence. The single dagaba, for example, was a mound of brickwork which would dominate St Paul's cathedral in London by over 15 metres (50 feet); and the *Jetawanarama dagaba* was constructed of sufficient brick to build a wall some 3 metres (10 feet) high, 0·3 metres (1 foot) wide, over 480 kilometres (300 miles) long . . .

Yet much of this splendour passed away also. An English seaman named Knox, who had been held captive in the Sinhalese mountains for twenty years, escaped in 1674 through the jungles which had grown around the ancient Anuradhapura, and his records convey the desolate beauty of the place. It was as though the city, for reasons which were not quite clear, had died completely. This once amazing centre – one of the finest in the entire world – had dwindled into a few huts around the sacred bodhi tree, in which a handful of monks lived as best they could surrounded by the jungle.

Then the city was partly discovered by British travellers, in the wake of the latest plunder and rapine of that wonderful land (perhaps a little more restrained than most), and after 1818 the lost city began to recover a trace of its old splendour. By 1888 the water supply was re-connected, a few roads had been rebuilt, and by the end of the century there was even a railway. Soon the city of Anuradhapura began to live once more, with a modern population inhabiting it like ghosts among a tattered fabric which whispers of the lost Golden Age of man.

branch of the bodhi tree at Gaya, the one under which Buddha attained his final illumination. The tree is now well over two thousand years old, and is still an object of pilgrimage and veneration.

A few miles outside the city is a huge stairway, partly cut into the rock, partly built of granite, which leads in 1840 steps up the 300 metres (1000 feet) of a steep rocky cliff to the monastery of Mihintale. This monastery was built in the second or third century, and

Pagan

View of the temple of Pagan, surrounded by jungle.

The traveller Captain Henry Yule, one of the first Englishmen to leave a description of the ancient city of Pagan, in Burma, wrote in the mid-nineteenth century that this place might pass for a scene set in another planet, 'so fantastic and unearthly was the architecture'. The buildings which stand there to this day support this view, yet these remains, remarkable as they are, must be a mere shadow of the city which the Mongol Kubla Khan found and destroyed in the thirteenth century. It stretched for at least 32 kilometres (20 miles) along the wide Irrawaddy river, and was said to contain over 13,000 pagodas alone!

Yet Kubla Khan was not the first to wreak destruction in this place. According to Burmese history, an ambassador from China was murdered while attending the Burmese King Naratheehapade, and in retaliation the Chinese Emperor invaded Burma. According to the Burmese, this army consisted of twenty million soldiers and six million horsemen, figures which lead one to suppose that the invasion itself was rooted in myth. The Chinese version of the story is actually recorded by the traveller Marco Polo, for he tells how the Chinese Emperor had such little respect for the Burmese that he sent against them an army composed chiefly of his court jesters. Whatever the truth about the invasion, the King of Burma decided to resist the Chinese, and in order to strengthen his capital he took the stones from many of the surrounding temples, destroying in the process 1000 large arched temples, 1000 small ones, and 4000 stupas! However, under one of the stupas his workmen found a prophetic inscription of doom, and as a result the king fled his newly reinforced city, and left his people to their fate.

One may well be tempted to see this account of the destruction of the temples in Pagan as being as exaggerated as the numbers of the Chinese hordes which these preparations were intended to resist, but this is probably not the case. When Captain Yule visited the site during the last century he left a very useful survey of what he found there; he counted over eight hundred temples, and estimated that there were probably still about a thousand within the space of the 13-kilometre (8-mile) strip which contains the remnants of this ancient city.

Captain Yule also described the enormous variety of the temple forms he found in Pagan. First, there were 'bell-shaped pyramids' of brickwork – effectively small versions of the stupas which abound in India to

this day. Secondly, related stupas, raised over square or octagonal cells, contained images of the Buddha. Thirdly, he found 'bluff knob-like domes, similar to the Sinhalese *dagaba*' (a word derived from the Sanscrit, meaning 'relic receptacle', and almost certainly the root for our own word 'pagoda'), which had a square cap, characteristic of the ancient Buddhist *caitya*. Most fantastic were the Bo-phya, the 'pumpkin pagodas', which, as Yule says, 'seemed rather like a fragment of what we might conceive the architecture of the moon than anything terrestrial'. But the

most common type was the cruciform vaulted temple.

The majority of these cruciform temples had fallen into disuse, 'abandoned to the owls and bats, and some have been dese-crated into cow-houses by the villagers', yet a few of the larger ones were still used for worship. Of these, Yule had no hesitation in describing the Ananda as the finest.

This temple is said to have been begun in the middle of the eleventh century by King Kyanzittha. According to tradition five Rahandahs, saints second in order only to a

Buddha, arrived at Pagan from the Himalayan region. It was from the description given by these of their own cave-temple that the Ananda was constructed, and indeed the name 'Ananda' is said to be used of the temple because it refers to the Nandamoola hills, from which the Rahandahs came (though it is popularly believed that the name refers to Ananda, the favourite cousin of the Buddha).

In the precincts around the Ananda was a large group of monastic buildings, forming a whole street, rich in wood carvings of warriors, dancers, spirits and *bibus* (the equivalent of ogres). The fretted pinnacles of the house ridges were topped with birds, cut in profile, in every attitude, sleeping, pecking, stalking or flying. Within the same street was a corridor with frescoes depicting the popular Jataka tales, intermixed with everyday scenes from Burmese life, and the many terrible punishments of the Buddhist hells. Demons are clubbing out the brains of sinners and hellish elephants trample upon their heads and yet of course the sinners 'live' to experience this punishment for their past immoralities.

From this medley of buildings, the traveller emerges to find himself before the gateway to the temple itself. The Ananda is in plan a square of nearly 60 metres (200 feet) in length, broken on each side by the projection of a large vestibule, which makes the building a perfect Greek cross. The central mass is about 9 metres (30 feet) high, with two tiers of windows, and above these is a series of roofs which look like sloping terraces, which then rise, almost organically, into the wonderfully carved supports for the spire which towers 50 metres (168 feet) above the ground.

Within this mass of masonry is a series of

Standing figures of Buddha in the Ananda temple.

124

dark concentric corridors, the central one of which leads to four huge chambers – lofty vaults some 15 metres (50 feet) high – in which four enormous golden statues of the Buddha stand, each about 9 metres (30 feet) high upon a lotus pedestal.

The most remarkable thing about these chambers is their special lighting, for the sunlight falls on to the Buddhas from above, from a recessed window in the second storey of the terraced roof. This light is totally unexpected in the gloomy confines of the temple, and it lends an unearthly radiance to the statues. Captain Yule was greatly struck by the effect: 'This unexpected and partial illumination in the dim recesses of these vaulted corridors produces a very powerful and strange effect, especially on the north side, where the front light through the great doorway is entirely subdued by the roofs of the covered approach of the monastic establishment.'

These strangely lighted Buddhas are said to be composed of different materials, each with a symbolic meaning. That to the east is the Buddha Kankathan, made of a sweet-scented wood. That to the west is the Kathaba, made of brass. To the north is the Gautama, made of fir, and to the south, the Ganno-goon, made of jasmine wood. In each case, however, the original material is covered with stucco which has been richly gilded.

This temple, like most of the temples in Pagan, is surrounded by a square enclosure. In the centre of the western vestibule, on an elevated and railed platform, is a representation of the Buddha's footprints, and in niches in the corridors running around the building are statues of Buddha, as well as numerous sculptured groups of figures intended to illustrate events in his life. The number of such groups and figures in this single temple has been estimated at over fifteen hundred, and yet the Ananda is only one of the hundreds of temples in this extraordinary place!

Some 400 metres (a quarter of a mile) to the south-west is another large temple, called the Thapinyu (next in size to the Ananda), which was built around AD 1100, and which is of a rather special design. The area under the 60-metre (200-foot) spire is actually hollowed out, and is used as a shrine for an enormous seated Buddha. The shrine room itself is not at ground level, but raised high upon a solid

foundation within the temple (so that the shrine may be entered only by way of a series of steep stairs), and the Buddha is seated within the chamber with his head at about the mid-point between the ground-work foundation and the pinnacle of the spire.

Among the earliest of the temples is the Manuha, which dates from 1059. It was built by the Mons, who governed Burma with Pagan as their capital until they were conquered in the mid-eleventh century. The pagoda at its core was completed by King Kyanzittha, and was to be a model for later Burman architecture.

Altogether, Pagan is one of the most remarkable cities ever built, and it is little wonder that Captain Yule should have been reduced to describing the buildings in terms of cosmic, lunar and other-worldly images, for even now, largely destroyed as it has been for nearly a thousand years, it still retains an unearthly aura.

The ornate and imposing exterior of the Ananda temple.

Borobudur

The world's most magnificent Buddhist *stupa*, or mound monument, is the Borobudur in central Java, set with a fine sense of drama against a backcloth of smoking volcanoes. Westerners often call this stupa a temple, but it is in fact a whole complex of shrines dedicated to the Buddha. It is still used to this day, by peasants who come to burn incense before the shrines, and to leave rose petals.

This stupa is the architectural masterpiece of Indonesian art, and was erected in the eighth century, under the Shailendra dynasty (AD 760–860). It is in effect a stone-covered hill, standing alone and imposing upon the plain: there are no remains of any city around the Borobudur, and it is quite possible that the stupa was built in such isolation, the site having no other purpose than Buddhist ritual.

From below, the Borobudur is an imposing dramatic structure, as complex in its symbolism or oriental cosmology as any work of art one is likely to find. From the air it looks something like a wedding cake iced by a manic baker. A less imaginative view of this fantastic structure might reasonably suggest that it is a sort of architectural mountain, which it is in more senses than one: the builders intended it to be a symbol of Mount Meru, which was supposed to exist at the central point of the earth. This mountain was said to be the dwelling place of the gods, the ancient 'Land of Bliss', the 'Golden Mountain' of legend. In the ravines of Mount Meru are to be found the bodies of human lovers who have failed to discover the true meaning of love.

In its basic form, the building has nine levels. This number is related to the somewhat complex numerical systems of Mahayanic Buddhist philosophy, which gave birth to this immense building. The four sides of the stone foundation are 150 metres (500 feet) long, and orientated to the four cardinal points. There is a ramp which provides

The lower terraces of the stupa at Borobudur. The steps in the foreground mark the start of the pilgrimage ascent.

access for pilgrims to climb up and around the pyramidal structure, a distance of some 5 kilometres (3 miles). The pilgrim may also walk around the base in a clockwise direction a prescribed number of times, from as few as three (still a not inconsiderable walk, in view of the size of this building) to as many as 108 times, which of course involves a prodigious effort! Of the nine levels, the first five are a series of tiers of decreasing squares, followed by three smaller concentrics, with a crowning stupa at the top.

This nine-fold division is deceptively simple, for it expresses certain of the most complex teachings connected with Buddhism. For a person used to the Western approach to symbolism, it is extremely difficult to reach into the mysteries which, so far as Buddhists are concerned, are quite clearly manifest in the Borobudur. It is almost impossible really to understand the significance and structure of the building by approaching it with the ordinary modern way of thinking, for its form embodies symbols which were designed for a different kind of mentality, and for a different age. An example of this, taken from a brief analysis of only one aspect of the Borobudur, may illustrate the difficulty we have of approaching it with ordinary Western consciousness.

The building may be seen as being divided into three quite separate (yet related) elements: there are the lower squares, the inner concentrics, and the crowning stupa, which is the *kailasa*, the 'centre of the cosmos', in which is embedded the totally hidden statue of the Buddha. While the significance of this single hidden Buddha has great importance in the tradition of the Mahayana branch of Buddhism, and the number five has also an important symbolism attached to it, it will be instructive for us to concentrate for the moment on the meaning of the three concentrics between the five and the one. Inevitably, this number three has a distinct relationship with the concept of the Trinity with which we in the West are more familiar, and for this reason alone it is worth looking more deeply into its meaning.

In the Buddhist symbolism, the three concentric circles relate to the teaching concerning the three 'developed' bodies of the Buddha, which are said to lie dormant in all human beings, but which were brought to perfection by the Buddha. In the Buddhist philosophy, these bodies are called the *dharma-kaya*, which means approximately 'glorified spiritual body', the *sambhoga-kaya*, which means 'body of compensation' and the *nirmana-kaya*, which is the 'transformed spiritual body'. These three bodies relate to the developed forms of the trinity within man which are called the Atman, Buddhi and Manas, about which there is a complex secret tradition concerning the destiny of man as a spiritual being.

Now it is perhaps sufficient to note that these three raised concentrics of the stupa have this significance, but in fact the number of small stupas which form these concentrics is also of considerable importance. These three circles are actually made up of seventy-two bell-like stupas which (as one may see through the holes in the lattice-work) contain images of Buddha – that is, forms of the Buddha in man which will be revealed in the future. This number seventy-two is a mystical number in both oriental and Western occult tradition. In man, who is seen as an image of the cosmos, the number is linked with the movement of his blood, for the pulse beats approximately seventy-two times every minute. In the heavens, this same number seventy-two is linked with the movement of the sun, for it takes precisely that number of years for the sun to drop back one degree against the backcloth of the stars in what is known as its precession. Thus, through this mystic number, the movement of the heart and the movement of the sun are united.

It is perhaps not essential that we grasp the full meaning of the symbolism of these seventy-two concentrics of partly hidden Buddhas, but it is interesting to observe that almost nothing in this vast edifice is left to chance: each element speaks volumes to those who know the language.

The lower galleries are said to contain over 1300 panels of relief sculptures depicting either incidents from the life of Buddha, symbolic references to his destiny, or stories from his previous incarnations. The lowest level of the base was originally sculpted with images of heaven and hell, but these were later covered over, perhaps in the same spirit as the topmost Buddha was hidden from ordinary sight. Stories from the life of Buddha were in the second layer, and illustrations from the more remarkable legends relating to his spiritual deeds in the third, while the fourth contained images relating to the Buddha who is to come in the future. The movement upwards, therefore, represents a spiritual liberation into future time, a movement away from the conditions of hell, through worldly existence into the sublime spiritual world, towards the hidden Buddha at the pinnacle.

We may see from such a brief glance at this symbolism why oriental historians should insist that this Borobudur is a 'Great Mandala'. The word 'mandala' is a Sanskrit term which means 'circle', but it has come to have special significance in the esoteric forms of Buddhism and Hinduism. Painted and woven mandalas are essentially abstract patterns which embody images of Buddhas and Boddhisattvas, and are used by monks as objects of meditation. Their vivid and con-centrically organized designs seem to be full of energy, which indeed they are for the monks who capture the forces available from them in their meditations.

A mandala is also a sacred precinct in honour of the Buddha or a Hindu deity. Like the graphic mandala it is an aid to self-realization, and, although it may be enclosed in a square or rectangle, is circular in shape. Both forms of mandala are symbolic diagrams of the cosmos and of man reflected in the cosmos. At the peak, but also at the centre, of this mandala of Borobudur is the concealed statue of the Buddha. The pilgrim who sets out to climb the clockwise direction around the stupa is setting out to reach this mystical centre. He is symbolically treading his own path, and the path of all Creation, to its own divine essence.

View of part of the circle of small stupas (each containing a partly visible statue of the Buddha) on the higher tiers of the stupa.

Angkor

The frontal approach to
the immense temple of
Angkor Wat.

The beautiful city of Angkor was deserted under mysterious circumstances around 1431 and began life again only in the last century when the French naturalist Henri Mouhot accidentally discovered it while cutting his way through the jungle. The city had been the sprawling capital of the ancient Khmer Empire, and even now, damaged by looting as much as by the roots of trees and luxuriant vegetation, contains over 600 temples, a dozen of which are as big as our European cathedrals, the largest being Angkor Wat.

King Jayavarman II first started to build Angkor in the ninth century, as the centre for the Hindu Khmer, whose empire was said to spread from Cambodia to modern Thailand and Vietnam. It was Jayavarman who put in hand the building of the canals and reservoirs which made possible the control of the rice-crop so that it gave three yields a year, and hence ensured the richness of the dynasty. A succession of kings built lakes and canals with the same sense of magnificence that they built their religious precincts, so that by the twelfth and thirteenth centuries the empire reached its zenith under the mighty rulers Suryavarman II and Jayavarman VII. The former not only extended the empire vastly, but also built the single temple for which the ancient race is most remembered – Angkor Wat.

Angkor Wat is 'a spectacle of beauty, wonder and magnificence', as the historian John Audric describes it, and certainly the greatest among the many glories of Khmer architecture and the masterpiece of Suryavarman II. This temple, like almost all related Hindu and Buddhist structures, was intended to be a model of the spiritual universe. The central pyramidal temple is meant to symbolize Mount Meru, which is in turn a symbol of the spiritual world of the gods. Its moated precinct represents Jambudvipa, which the Khmers believed to be the central continent of the world, and the 4-kilometre (2½-mile)

circumference of the Angkor Wat walls was a symbol of the edge of the world, with eight guardian spirits at the cardinal points.

Forming a huge series of lotus-bud towers the central block of the temple has a base 215 by 186 metres (717 by 620 feet) and a height of 60 metres (200 feet), but this is enclosed within a series of precincts which measure 1500 by 1200 metres (5000 by 4000 feet). The overall effect of the building is one of bewildering profusion of terraces, galleries, towers and courtyards, standing within an immense moat or artificial lake, 180 metres (600 feet) wide.

This huge moat – with floating islands of luxuriant and colourful flowers – reminds us that Angkor was literally founded upon water, for the ancient city of Angkor Thom,

as the adjacent city is called, was constructed upon a complex network of canals and lakes. Angkor Thom was the capital of the empire, and was surrounded by three huge reservoirs, with a water surface of about the same area as the land it fed and supported. Over sixty huge canals within this area alone may be counted from the reconstructed plans, though most of these are now dried up and choked with vegetation.

A description of this magnificent canal system, when still in operation, is provided for us by a Portuguese chronicler, Diogo do Couto, who lived in Goa in India in the late seventeenth century: 'The water enters by the two gates on the north and east sides, and then flows back into the moat from the south and east [gates], so that the water in the moat never diminishes, for whatever quantity enters from the two gates returns outside by the other two. As for the great moat, it is always full, since important, well-stocked rivers empty into it. In fact, the excess of water made it necessary to build a number of outlets so that the moat would not run over. So it is that each one of the roads that leaves the gates is flanked by another two [canals] which are used by a multitude of boats. These latter come from the interior of the country along its outer rivers, laden with provisions, firewood, and other commodities. And the city's garbage is removed the same way, hauled outside as far as the moat, so that after the king had discovered the city and transferred his court there, it became the most beautiful, the best served, and cleanest city in the world.'

Angkor Thom was designed to rule and administer a total population within the city and in the surrounding extra-mural houses and precincts of nearly two million people. To enter it, one crosses the moat by way of the south-gate causeway which is 'guarded' by rows of stone gods and demons, of which it is said there are 540 around the city. The enclosure of the city was at one time occupied by the royal apartments and those of the religious dignitaries and priests, its two main areas being the Grand Plaza, a ceremonial centre for naval and military reviews, and a magnificent temple called the Bayon in the centre.

The central temple of Bayon is a famous 'visage-tower', built at the end of the thirteenth century by Jayavarman VII, a con-

Details of the royal heads on the towers of Bayon at Angkor Thom.

fusion of decorated wall surfaces and carved faces on the outside producing an undulating organic richness of texture which gives the impression that the building is itself alive. For all its religious intent, there is something forboding about it. There is in Bayon, as indeed in Angkor Wat, a sense of intensity, of what John Audric described as 'an uneasy feeling of being watched'. It is as though the vast stone faces upon the buildings, said to be portraits of Jayavarman VII, which peer down at one on every side are still imbued with the spiritual agencies which the ancient Khmer believed could dwell in stone. The strange feeling may be linked with the history of this period of Khmer greatness, for it is recorded that the slaves who built the crypts and walls of Bayon were murdered and buried under the outer walls, and even the high priests had their tongues cut out, so that the secrets of the architecture – and of the treasures buried within the building – might not be revealed.

Such stories, although perhaps apocryphal, remind us that Khmer society was slave-based. As with so many of the early cultural centres, the greatness of Angkor depended upon the strength of a god-king cult which was founded on the idea that the king, if not actually a god himself, was directly and personally responsible to the gods. The gods, in turn, were interested in the welfare of the earth in general, and in the race ruled by that god-king in particular. Thus, Angkor Wat and the later Angkor Thom were built by hordes of slaves essentially in the service of a religious cult – mainly around Siva, but to some extent around Buddha – as Jayavarman VII, who built Angkor Thom, was a Buddhist sympathizer. The god-king cult inevitably had powerful social consequences: society was polarized, and there were terrible slave and worker revolts which were in every case put down most cruelly.

The important cult of the god-king was given an external symbolism in the 'creative power' associated with the *linga*, relating to the cult of Siva. A linga was a representation of a phallus, popularly seen now only as a sexual object, but in fact of considerable spiritual significance, and each ruler was expected to build a new capital around one. This symbol was to be raised on a hill, either natural or man-made, upon which was to be erected a temple, which was in turn to be the centre of a city. Although the ideal was not strictly adhered to by all the Khmer god-kings, we find an impressive example here in the Bayon, situated within the confines of Angkor Thom.

Many of the findings of modern archaeologists have been supported by a curious first-hand report made by a Mongol-Chinese envoy sent to Angkor in 1296, which gives a fascinating and detailed account of the rich life of the ruling Khmer at that time. His description of the city is one which might have been written recently, so well preserved are the things of which he writes: 'Beyond the wall is a wide moat, which is traversed by way of five causeways. On each side of the bridge are fifty-four gigantic and frightening statues of gods, with bridge parapets constructed in the form of two enormous snakes, each with nine heads, their bodies supported by the giants. Above each gate there are five stone Buddhas, each with their faces turned towards the cardinal points. Elephants are sculpted on the stone doors, the ramparts of the walls are built of enormous blocks, and trees have been planted along these ramparts. Within the huge walls are more gates, which are closed at night and well guarded by sentries. Dogs, as well as criminals who have had their toes cut off, are not allowed inside these gates. A golden tower stands at the centre of this city, flanked by more than twenty stone towers and hundreds of houses. A bridge of gold stretches from the East Gate, and two golden lions have been placed on each side of this bridge, whilst eight golden Buddhas stand below the stone galleries . . . The eastern lake is just over a mile from the walled city: in the middle of this is a stone Buddha, who has water perpetually flowing from out of his navel.'

Detail of relief carvings which make up the ornate exterior decoration of the temple at Angkor Wat.

CHINA
AND
JAPAN

Great bronze statue of the Buddha at Kamakura,
Japan, made in 1252.

The Great Wall of China

When, through one of the great wonders of the modern world, it became possible to take photographs of our earth from the moon, the only man-made construction which was visible at that distance was the Great Wall of China, a thin scratch across a continental mass. Although its foundations were laid over two thousand years ago, it is still the longest permanent defence system ever made by man.

It is difficult to say precisely how long this wall is – accounts vary, depending upon how it is measured. Some authorities claim that it is 2400 kilometres (1500 miles) long; others put it at 3200 kilometres (2000 miles), or even twice that distance. Difficulties in measuring arise from the fact that it is no longer complete (though parts of it have been very skilfully restored in recent times). When it was first made into one long wall, in the third century BC, it stretched from the Gulf of Chili, in the Yellow Sea, over high mountain terrain, along the north frontier of China, to Chiayukuan in the west. It was said to have been defended along its length by 30,000 towers, its meandering loops stretching 6400 kilometres (4000 miles), though defending a crow-flight distance of some 3200 kilometres (2000 miles).

Before the third century fairly long stretches of defensive wall did exist along the frontier; these had been built by various feudal lords to keep back the raiding horsemen from the north. However, when the remarkable 'Universal Emperor', Shih Huang Ti, a revolutionary, far-seeing and utterly fanatical man, founded the short-lived Ch'in dynasty in 221 BC, and began to weld together the first unified China, it became evident from the frequent raids from the north that something would have to be done to strengthen these defences. The raiders were the Hiunghu, the fierce and terrible ancestors of the later Huns, who plagued and terrorized the Romans under Attila.

Towards this end, Shih Huang Ti began one of the most vast and unpopular building schemes ever devised by man – the reinforcing of the old walls, and the construction of new fortifications to make one long sweep of wall, protected by a chain of fortifications by which it was possible to maintain a permanent communication with the city. The building of the wall was of course accompanied by the building of a vast network of sophisticated road systems to serve it.

This wall was some 4·5 to 9 metres (15 to 30 feet) high in most places, but in difficult terrain it was sometimes as high as 15 metres (50 feet). It was between 4·5 and 7·5 metres (15 to 25 feet) wide in most places – certainly wide enough to allow groups of men, from small contingents to whole armies, to have rapid and unhampered access along the whole length.

The linked defensive towers were placed at very frequent intervals, a metre or so higher and wider than the wall, with living accommodation within. In places the wall was made from hard-stamped earth faced with stone brickwork, but in the more vulnerable places it was made of solid-built stone. The system of defensive towers was linked with a complex beacon system for 'early warning' of attacks from the north, the signalling being done by smoke during the day, and by fires at night.

What made the building of the wall so unpopular was the fact that it had to be done by hundreds of thousands of conscripts, who were moved from their homes against their will, and who had to work under the most terrible conditions. Many thousands of men died through overwork and bad planning. Huang Ti has gone down in history for more than merely the building of the wall and the first unification of China, but also for his autocratic burning of the books ('knowledge is dangerous'). Not surprisingly, the walls were built for reasons which were also politi-

The Great Wall of China, snaking its way along the northern frontiers.

cal, for they not only retained lands overrun by the Ch'in themselves, but united an expansionist policy with a wish to determine for all time the extent of the new unified China. The wall did indeed contribute towards this latter aim – not only did it serve to some extent its explicit purpose of holding back the Steppes horsemen and the terrible Hiung-hu, but in 'containing' China it helped to give a sense of unity to the vast and multifarious kingdom.

In comparison with the stupendous labour involved in the building of a wall of this kind, the most famous walls in Europe are relatively pathetic affairs. The best-known still standing, the wall of Hadrian, which was originally intended to divide England from Scotland, is only 117 kilometres (73 miles) long, with a height of about 5 metres (16 feet), and a thickness of 2·5 metres. The Romans, being magnificent engineers, did build much longer walls – for example the Limes Germanicus, which ran from Neuwied (near the Rhine) to the Danube, ending near Ratisbon, was nearly 480 kilometres (300 miles) long – but not even the Romans built anything which approached the scale of this Great Wall of China.

The Imperial City, Peking

In Peking it is as though the Chinese dragon has taken to its wings, and flown into the heavens, for it was here that the ancient arts of China reached their supreme expression in dedication to the ancestor cult, and to the man-god emperor. It is in Peking that one may see written the whole history of the Chinese world, with its slow and often bloody change from absolute autocracy to a struggle for unified brotherhood. This political centre of China has been sacked, demolished, ruled and misruled by natives and foreigners alike, its people killed and tortured in the pursuance of dynastic struggles. Even in the past thousand years, the city has been totally destroyed and rebuilt four times, which is perhaps why it is called 'the Phoenix City', the *peking*, ever reborn anew from the fires.

The first of the vast destructions was that ordered by the Mongol leader Genghis Khan. Even he waited for two years outside the barrier of the Great Wall, appeased somewhat by Chinese gifts, but finally, in 1215, at the price of terrible losses, he broke through the walls to Peking itself, and razed the city to the ground. His troops killed all the men and raped the women, so that the Khan might indulge his greatest joy, which was to seize the property of his enemies, and 'see their families in tears, ride their horses, and possess their daughters and wives'.

His grandson, Khubla Khan, rebuilt Peking, along with his new Winter Palace, and called it Tai Tu, 'the Great Capital'. By the end of the century it had indeed become one of the greatest capitals ever seen, with a population of over half a million, defended behind walls ten kilometres (six miles) long, behind which was another vast walled square, well guarded by strong towers. It was this fabled city which the Venetian traveller Marco Polo visited in 1275, returning to Europe years later with stories which few men believed, about the Chinese palace built in gold. His stories sparked off the young

Columbus, who sought to sail westwards to this Cathay, but who reached another great continent, where there were other palaces filled with gold.

Old Peking is still something like a Chinese puzzle box, for it consists of a large box containing smaller boxes, which in turn contain other boxes. The inner city is adjacent to the outer city, these being called respectively the 'Tartar' and the 'Chinese' cities, the former being the old centre of the Manchu administration. This in turn encloses the walls of the ancient Imperial City, which further encloses the famous 'Forbidden City'.

Taking the smallest box first, the Forbidden City is surrounded by ancient walls marking off an area of about 900 by 990 metres (3000 by 3300 feet), beautifully faced in glazed purple bricks, and roofed with yellow tiles. This Forbidden City is divided into a number of smaller walled areas, all serving the needs of the Imperial Palace – the living quarters, the houses of the palace ladies, the shrines and temples. A five-port gateway, the Wu Men, leads into the Imperial City.

The next box is that of the Imperial City itself. This vast area is distinguished by its three large artificial lakes, and again by many temples and official houses.

The box holding these two is the Tartar City, which lies to the north of modern Peking, with a perimeter wall of about 24 kilometres (15 miles), approximately in the form of a square, in places some 12 metres (40 feet) high. Within this area are several very beautiful temples, and a tower with a forty-tonne bell.

The adjacent Chinese city has within it the most famous of all buildings in Peking: the religious precinct of the Temple of Heaven and its related Altar of Heaven; we shall look at these in a little more detail shortly.

Ancient maps of the more intrepid travellers who ventured into old Cathay, and even

View through one of the major gates into the Forbidden City of Peking.

External view of one of the huge halls of the Imperial Palace in the Forbidden City.

reached Peking, show many of the features of the two larger cities, but the information relating to the inner square of the Forbidden City is scant. The high walls of the city are usually shown, perhaps with an indication of the two deflected streams from the Golden River which flow through the walls, and one of which is crossed by lovely marble bridges; but in general that is all. So enclosed was this city, so hidden from ordinary eyes, that the map-makers had to leave the square empty of architectural details. When the European map-makers reached areas of land which remained unexplored, and around which legends had been built, they often also left those parts empty, and wrote nearby the eternal warning: 'Here there be dragons'. Such a phrase could well have been written over this empty square of the Forbidden City, for here indeed was the Dragon Throne, from which ancient justice was dispensed to the surrounding world.

This Forbidden City is said to lie on the central point of the earth, in a China whose very name translates 'Middle of the World'. Thus, no undue boasting was involved when the Chinese emperor, seated on the awful Dragon Throne in the Hall of Supreme Harmony – a lonely and totally alienated figure – should choose to describe himself as 'Lord of the Universe'. His word was indeed inflexible law, his every whim immediately catered for: a sign of the smallest displeasure would inevitably lead to the mutilation or death of another human being, a nod from him might unleash an army of a quarter of a million men.

With all this concern for the 'centre', Europeans are sometimes surprised to find that Chinese logic does not locate the precise point within the palace itself, or over the Dragon Throne. The supposed centre of the world lies, in fact, in or on a man-made hill, just north of the palace walls. The hill was located and designed in accordance with the magical practices of the Chinese system of *feng shui*, for which there is no equivalent European form, and which was concerned with the occult manipulation of earth-forces and earth-spirits for the benefit of man and his environment.

The actual 'manipulative' centre, from which the emperor dispensed his justice or injustice – the audience palace – has been described as the showpiece of this group of buildings in Peking. In fact, there are three different audience rooms within the building, each intended to serve various functions, but deriving from the ancient Chinese decree (at least as old as the Chou dynasty) that the Son of Heaven should rule from three courts. The resulting halls are known as the T'ai ho tien, which spans an area of about 30 by 90 metres (100 by 300 feet) and is intended for mass audiences, the Chung ho tien, which has a pyramidal roof, and the Pao ho tien, intended for vast state banquets.

The Wu Men, with its immense bronze lions, looks on to the Hall of Supreme Harmony, which is 60 metres (200 feet) wide and 30 metres (100 feet) deep, orientated on the south–north axis as important Chinese buildings should be. The ramped gatehouse of the Hall of Supreme Harmony has before it a curved stream, deflected from the Golden River, which is crossed by five marble bridges, originally designed to accommodate the complex protocol of the processions of the emperor. In front of this is a huge square, which has in modern times become the Chinese equivalent of the New York Times Square, or of Trafalgar Square in London,

Bronze Fu-dog, often called a lion, in front of the Gate of Supreme Harmony.

that is, a gathering place for ordinary people.

The most sacred of all Chinese buildings, the Altar of Heaven, lies in the outer, 'Chinese', city. It consists of three enormous circular marble terraces, with four groups of steps directed towards the cardinal points. These concentrics are situated in a huge square, surrounded by another circle, the whole ground-plan designed to reflect the Chinese magical numbers system. This altar is linked to the circular temple by a 400-metre (quarter-mile) raised causeway which leads to the most famous of all buildings in Peking, the Temple of Heaven, with its triple tier of cobalt glazed tiles, and marble balustrades. The building is 30 metres (99 feet) high, and is supported by columns of the nanmu tree. The inside of the wonderful cupola is of wood, painted in exquisite golds, reds, yellows and oranges. Unfortunately, it was destroyed by fire at the end of the last century, and the present building is a detailed reconstruction.

Once upon a time, in that fairyland and nightmare which was China, the emperor dwelt within the walls of the Forbidden City, with its hundreds of gardens, ponds, rivers and pagodas – all of distinctive workmanship and artistic merit – amidst rooms which might be large enough to gather 10,000 people to pay homage to this god-king, or tiny enough for meditation, where one might be quite alone for reflection on a work of art. Today one might spend months exploring this place, lost among names which translate into the language of romance: the Pavilion of the Purest Perfume, the Palace of Earthly Tranquillity, the Pavilion of Depth of Knowledge, the Pavilion of Floating Jade, and even the House of Fairies.

Within this complex of delights lived an emperor who for all his power had less freedom than almost any human being in the modern world. Virtually every movement was ordained by others, by ritual and custom. In the spring he lived in the Eastern Palace, wore green clothes and ate wheat bread and lamb; in summer he lived in the Southern Palace, wore white clothes and ate that delicacy, dog meat; in the autumn . . . and so on. His political decisions were made for him by the vast retinue of mandarins, and even his private life was strictly controlled. He was perhaps the loneliest man in the world in the midst of all these pleasure palaces.

Horyu-ji

The religious precinct of Horyu-ji is a master-piece of art and architecture produced by an age when life had a great dignity and meaning. The centre has been likened in its nobility to the Acropolis in Athens, but Horyu-ji has one great advantage over the Greek site in that its buildings are still well-preserved today.

Horyu-ji dates from the seventh century, and marks a great creative surge which preceded and anticipated the time in the history of Japan which is known as the Nara period. Although lasting only a short length of time, from AD 710 to 794, the Nara period was perhaps the most creative of all periods in Japanese history. As with many things Japanese, it involved the assimilation of foreign excellence – in this case the best of Chinese art and architecture – but this influence was absorbed and transformed into something unique.

The city of Nara, nowadays a series of modern buildings interspersed with religious precincts, was a huge and teeming capital during this expansive period. It is now a relatively quiet place, shaken awake at times by the tourist industry, which seems to be steadily tightening its stranglehold on Japan. Nara's tranquil spirituality contrasts strongly with the horror of the modern amusement park nearby (appropriately called 'Dream-land'), a place of which even the guidebooks show signs of being ashamed.

And yet there are still so many ancient beauties and delights which remain. The most striking of these are to be found in the Kofuku-ji and Todai-ji temples. The Kofuku-ji, originally built in AD 710, but destroyed and rebuilt many times, comprises pagodas, treasure halls, and temples. Nearby is the Nara Park, impressive in its natural beauty, and adjacent to it is the Todai-ji temple, which contains the famous Daibutsuden (see next section).

About 11 kilometres (7 miles) out of Nara is the religious precinct of Horyu-ji, in which is preserved much that is of a finer quality than that found at Nara (with the exception of Todai-ji). Because the Japanese learned to specialize in building from wood, and because these early craftsmen, like all great artists of the past, built to last for ever, this Horyu-ji has some of the earliest known wooden buildings in the world (although the very oldest is the Shoso-in, again in Todai-ji).

The precinct of Horyu-ji is usually called a temple, although in fact it is a complex series of buildings designed to serve religious purposes, and within the whole area are thirty-three buildings, erected between the century before the Nara period and the Edo period (1615–1868). It is certainly the most important architectural centre in Japan, and it is possibly for this reason that the founder of this precinct, Shotoku, is immortalized in portrait form on the modern banknotes of the country.

The reconstruction of the original Horyu-ji is a somewhat difficult matter, but the drawing to the right gives some idea of the central temple precinct. The inner lecture hall, united to a colonnaded walk (furthest from the two-tiered gateway), behind which stood the northern dormitory, was removed a long time ago. The colonnade was then extended to accommodate two small buildings to either side of the rear of the lecture hall, to run into a

The Kondo, or Golden Hall (*above*), and the five-storey pagoda in the temple precinct (*above right*).
Right Perspective view of the precinct, showing the Kondo (in the middle of the precinct) and the pagoda (to its left).

new colonnaded hall over the site of the dormitory itself. However, apart from this major modification the courtyard of the Horyu-ji remains much the same as it must have appeared in the Nara period.

The precinct now consists of two main areas: the western area, which holds the Kondo, or Golden Hall, and the pagoda; and the eastern area, which contains the pavilion, the Yume dono, and the nunnery, or Chugu-ji.

The Kondo, which was originally built about AD 607, seems from the outside to consist of two floors, but the upper storey is a false one, serving only to increase the height of the building when viewed from within. In the central space is a platform for holy images, a few of which have been moved to the Treasure Hall. Originally the famous Yakushi, the 'healing Buddha', was in this hall, made, as the inscription on the halo tells, in order to cure the illness of the Emperor

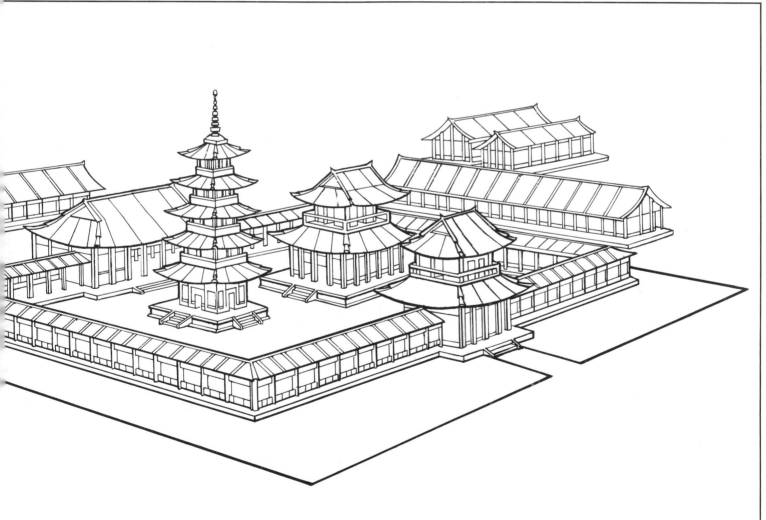

Yomei; it is now in the Treasure Hall, with many other great works of art which were scattered in buildings throughout the Horyu-ji.

One of the most remarkable works of art which has been removed from the Kondo is a magnificent 'Beetle-winged Shrine', the Tama-mushi Zushi, made from cypress wood, painted in lacquer. This is also to be found in the Treasure Hall, and takes its name from the fact that the metalwork edging was once inset with the iridescent wings of beetles which glowed and scintillated in the light – a technique which appears to have come to Japan (like Buddhism itself) from Korea. The shrine is profusely decorated, with scenes from the life and previous lives of Buddha.

One of the more remarkable of these stories, told in 'continuous representation' by which several separate incidents from the same story are depicted in the same space, in a kind of telescoping of time, is the so-called 'sacrifice for a stanza'. This story recounts how in a previous incarnation the Buddha was a Brahmin whom the god Indra decided to test and instruct. The god disguised himself as a demon, who then recited to the Buddha-Brahmin half of a verse (or stanza) which went: 'All component things are transitory. The Law is to be born and die . . .' Of course, the Buddha-Brahmin was anxious to hear the complete verse, for the pronouncement as it stood was fairly bleak. The demon at this point slyly explained that he could live only on human flesh, but added that for such a meal he would be able to recall the complete verse. Buddha promised immediately that he would sacrifice his own flesh in order to hear the missing part of the stanza. This turned out to be virtually the message of Buddhism, for it ran 'transcending birth and death, how blissful is the absolute'. Having heard this, the Buddha promptly sacrificed himself to the demon. His death proved to be symbolic of his future Buddhahood, for he threw himself down from a high tree, and it was under a tree, the bodhi, that he gained illumination in his final incarnation.

The Kondo once upon a time housed the most wonderful Buddhist frescoes, but these were almost entirely destroyed by fire in 1949, and have now been replaced by good quality reproductions where necessary.

The pagoda stands upon a double stone foundation, some 32 metres (108 feet) high, with a series of five glazed tile roofs which reduce in width in such a proportion that the top storey is exactly half the width of the bottom one. Pagodas were a later development serving a similar function to stupas (see for example page 104), but they were far less stable than mounds of stone masonry, being designed to withstand earthquakes in a most ingenious manner. In their simplest form they may be thought of as a series of elongated cups resting upside-down on a huge central pillar; such an arrangement allows a swaying motion, without leading to the whole edifice collapsing. Under the central pillar of this particular pagoda in Horyu-ji is said to be buried one of the bones of Buddha.

Leading to the eastern sector of the precinct is the Todaimon, an eight-pillared gateway, behind which is a temple built in AD 737 on the site of the destroyed palace of Prince Shotoku. In this is the famous Yume dono, the 'Hall of Dreams', in which a lost image of Kwannon, the goddess of mercy, was found by the American Ernest Fenellosa in 1884. This lovely statue of the goddess is regarded as one of the masterpieces of early sculpture, with her slender proportions which carry her beyond the ordinary world of man. The figure is made of wood, but painted in gold-leaf.

North of the main hall is the Chugu-ji nunnery, in which is lodged another statue of the same goddess, the Nyorin Kwannon, as well as the oldest piece of embroidery in Japan, the 'Tapestry of Heaven', said to have been sewn by a princess.

Horyu-ji is one of the finest products of the early period of Japanese Buddhism. The religion was officially introduced into Japan from Korea in AD 552, and was furthered by the wisdom of Prince Shotoku, who saw in its religious tenets and morality a new ground for Japanese spiritual and political expansion. Through Buddhism a new impulse was given to ordinary education, and it also brought a deepening of the morality which is the basis of all healthy societies. By clever, but quite honourable manipulation, Shotoku managed to have the native Shintoism of Japan absorbed into Buddhism, thus avoiding the religious schisms which might have split the country. The Emperor Shomu, who reigned AD 724–48, decreed that a Buddhist monas-

Detail of a fresco from the Nara period (AD 710–94) at Horyu-ji.

Hinayana, which means 'Little Vehicle' – which flourished in southern India and Ceylon. Theravada Buddhism is more purist in adhering to the Buddha's teachings.) Various sects and tendencies of Mahayana Buddhism followed to Japan and quickly took root. The first great wave came with the establishment of six different schools from China during the Nara period: the Sanron, the Hosso, the Kegon, the Ritsu, the Jojitsu and the Kusha. These were separated by differences which were predominantly intellectual in character, and revolved around the questions of whether the material universe is real or unreal, to what extent, if any, Buddhahood is available to all living creatures, and the value of ritual. The adherents of the early sects of Japanese Buddhism were mainly from the court circles around the emperor. Later other forms of Buddhism developed, which were more accessible to ordinary people. The best known of these to-day are the Jodo and the Zen varieties. Followers of the widespread Jodo sect believe that the chanting of the name of the Buddha Amida is sufficient to gain rebirth into the realms of pure bliss. In contrast, Zen, the form of Buddhism most associated in the West with Japan, imposes an austere discipline with considerable emphasis on meditation and the transcending of ordinary ways of thinking.

The widespread acceptance of Buddhism, at least among the ruling classes, and its readiness to adopt through assimilation certain Japanese characteristics, had an incalculable effect on the growth of the nation. By bringing harmony and peace to a nation riven by warring clans it achieved what Prince Shotoku desired through its ideals and strictures for fulfilled existence. Ten precepts and six 'perfections' are at the root of Buddhist morality. The precepts are: (i) not to take life, (ii) not to steal, (iii) not to have unlawful sexual intercourse, (iv) not to lie, (v) not to talk frivolously, (vi) not to slander, (vii) not to be double-tongued, (viii) not to be covetous, (ix) not to be malicious, and (x) not to be heretical. This last precept is directed towards maintaining unity within the 'three treasures' of the Buddha, the Law, and the Congregation. The six perfections are the exercise of (i) charity, (ii) morality, (iii) patience, (iv) fortitude, (v) meditation, and (vi) knowledge.

tery and nunnery should be built in every province throughout the Empire, and it was this which led to the building of the huge Daibutsuden in Nara.

Horyu-ji dates from the earliest period of Buddhist building in Japan. With the great impetus given by Prince Shotoku Buddhist temples and other religious buildings sprang up across the country, to such an extent that by AD 624 Japan had forty-six Buddhist monasteries. The number continued to grow at a rapid rate, so that there were 545 monasteries and temples by only AD 692.

The monks who built and studied at Horyu-ji derived their religion from China, where the branch of Buddhism known as Mahayana, or 'Great Vehicle', flourished. (The other branch is the Theravada – or

Todai-ji

The temple of Todai-ji in Nara was one of the finest Buddhist precincts in the world, with its lovely gatehouse, two superb pagodas (each with their own walled areas) and the central building of the Daibutsu-den, which holds the bronze statue of Buddha, the largest in the world. The height of the Buddha alone is 16 metres (53 feet), and including the lotus pedestal it comes to over 21 metres (71 feet). Over 435 tonnes of copper went into the bronze founding, and it weighs 560 tonnes. It is almost impossible to gain an idea of the vast size of this figure from photographs, or from mere measurements: we might grasp something of its scale if we realize that the ear alone is much bigger than a human being, with its length of 2·5 metres (8 feet 5 ins), and that two tall men, holding hands, might just manage to stretch across its enormous face. The Buddha is seated on a lotus flower of a thousand petals, each petal of which is said to represent an entire universe, with each universe peopled with countless smaller worlds. Worlds within worlds, reminding us of the *sutra* which says, 'in every particle of dust there are present Buddhas without number'.

According to popular tradition this Daibutsu was erected to counteract the plague which was ravaging the area in AD 735. In fact, the real reason for its construction was the wish of the priests to celebrate the union which had been forged (under the direction of the Emperor Shomu Tenno) between the native Shinto religion and Buddhism, which had come to Japan via Korea in the sixth century.

The curious ceremony of 'eye-opening' which marked the dedication of the Great Buddha in 752 was a vast pageant headed by the Empress Koken (the same who gave the world the earliest known surviving example of printing – an art learned from China). The actual ceremony was performed by an Indian monk named Bohisena, who brushed a film of water over the eyes of the Buddha. A long string had been attached to the brush and this was passed through the hands of those in the hall, in order that they might participate in this act of bringing the statue to life.

The history of the Buddha has not been quite so peaceful as his appearance might suggest. In AD 855 his huge head fell off and was replaced only with the greatest difficulty. Then, in 1180, during the civil wars, the Daibutsu-den was burned down and the flames were so hot that the head of the Buddha melted. It was restored some fifteen years later, the cost of restoration being raised by the monk Jugen who travelled through Japan with a wheelbarrow, collecting coins. After another period of anarchy, the hall was once more burned down by vandals, and the Buddha sat in the open for almost a century. After such adventures, and several restorations, it is unlikely that much of the original bronze remains, though the figure probably retains much of the original design.

The temple which holds the Great Buddha is said to be the largest wooden building under one roof in the world. It is 48 metres (160 feet) high, 56 metres (187 feet) long, and 50 metres (166 feet) wide. The present building is actually an early eighteenth-century restoration, made when feudal anarchy led to the original being destroyed. This restoration was not done in the best possible taste, and the building is not as extensive as it was.

The imperial temple at Todai-ji actually became the prototype for very many other temples in Japan. The Emperor Shomu, anxious to spread Buddhism throughout the land, ordered that each province within the country should build a temple and religious precinct, along the lines of the Todai-ji, in honour of Buddha.

This Emperor Shomu, who did much to extend the new religion through Japan, is linked with one of the greatest material gifts

The Great Buddha in the Daibutsu-den.

ever made – an entire Imperial treasure. When he died, his wife was so stricken with grief that she decided to make an offering to Buddha. She presented the entire Imperial collection of wonderful statues, silk fabrics, paintings, ceramics, costumes, armour, swords, chests of jewels (60,000 precious stones alone have been counted) and many fine works of art. The record of this gift is still in existence, and is perhaps one of the saddest love letters of all time: 'Forty-nine days have passed since the day of the death of my beloved master, but every day my passion grows and the pain makes my heart heavier. Supplicating the Earth or calling the Sky does not bring me any consolation. And I have decided to do good deeds to give joy to his respected spirit. And for this reason I give these treasures to Buddha so that the soul of the Emperor may rest in peace.'

CENTRAL
AND
SOUTH
AMERICA

Great Pyramid, dedicated to Quetzalcoatl,
at Chichen Itza.

Teotihuacan

When the amazed Spaniards first laid eyes on the city of Teotihuacan, their Aztec guides assured them that it had been built by giants, and showed them the huge thigh-bones of these mighty constructors. The thigh-bones in fact proved later to be those of elephants, but sight of this extraordinary place still persuades one that only giants could have built it.

Teotihuacan is said by some archaeologists to be the earliest of the pre-Columbian civilizations in Central America, dating as it does from at least 100 BC. However, the sophistication of its architecture and art forms would suggest that this was no mere 'beginning' in human culture, but part of a regular flow. Perhaps those people who claim that such

The massive pyramidal Temple of the Sun at Teotihuacan. Its base area is even larger than that of the Great Pyramid in Egypt.

centres were the later forms (indeed, the degenerate forms) of a vast civilization which flourished in ancient Atlantis are not quite so misguided as is generally supposed!

The city lies about 40 kilometres (25 miles) north-east of Mexico City. At the height of its culture, it appears to have sprawled over an area of 20 square kilometres (about 8 square miles), although the existing remains of the religious structures now cover a much smaller area of a relatively narrow strip, 3 kilometres (2 miles) in length.

Almost everything we know about this ancient city is derived from the Aztecs, but it was already a mystery by their time, so that even the names of the main buildings within the complex are a matter of guesswork. The names given to the three most outstanding

buildings in the area, the Temples of the Sun and Moon, and the Citadel, are obviously of Aztec origin. Although the Aztecs may have derived the use of these temples from the Oltecs, the people who built them, we are basically ignorant of their true names and functions.

The so-called pyramid Temple of the Sun, which rises in four stages to a height of 65 metres (216 feet), on a square plane of 210 metres (700 feet), and which covers a larger area than even the Great Pyramid of Egypt (see page 20), was at one time surmounted by a temple. We may therefore regard the pyramid itself as a gigantic stairway – certainly, quite unlike the Egyptian pyramids, it was designed to be climbed, and for the worshippers to approach the temple through physical effort and (presumably) in keeping with prescribed religious rituals. There is no evidence that the worship was in any way connected with the sun, however.

Similarly, the pyramid of the Moon temple, which stands 42 metres (140 feet) high, may not have had any real connection with moon cults. It was said by the Aztecs to have been surmounted by a huge stone figure relating to the moon, but this figure was later unearthed (weighing 22 tonnes, which must have somehow been man-handled to the top of the pyramid), and it is thought more likely that it represented a water deity.

Even more off the mark is the term 'Citadel' when applied to the enclosure which contains the temples and other religious buildings, for there is absolutely no evidence that the Oltecs who built this city intended their walls to be defended at all. The main building in this precinct is indeed a temple which was probably dedicated to the strange plumed serpent god Quetzalcoatl. The modern name 'citadel' appears to have been derived from the fact that the Spaniards used it precisely as such, having their cannon drawn up to the top, from which point they could survey with safety the whole area.

A long and straight processional road runs from the river to the Temple of the Moon – a road called 'the Way of the Dead' by the Aztecs, though there is no reason to believe that this is what the Oltecs called it, over 2000 years ago, when they constructed this city. This processional roadway has a wide axis, and is over two kilometres long (about a mile and a half). It was stone paved and with

The Temple of the Moon at the northern end of the 'Avenue of the Dead' at Teotihuacan.

several stepped terraces, so that a slow approach from the river towards the Temple of the Moon would have given the impression that the pyramid ahead was at one moment sinking in the ground, the next moment rising over the horizon. Perhaps indeed it was this 'rising and setting' illusion which led the Aztecs to link the pyramid with the moon in the first place. Actually, this particular pyramid, with its base of 215 metres (710 feet) square, is orientated in such a way as to face directly towards the setting sun. It would have been more imposing in its original form, for the temple which was constructed on the top would have taken it much higher than the present 64 metres (212 feet). There is a kind of piazza at the second level of this truncated pyramid, from which the steps lead towards the vast ritual stairway, reminding us that few if any of the American temple complexes should be called pyramids for they are really raised temple supports.

The so-called Citadel is accessible from the west by means of a broad stairway which runs at right-angles to the Way of the Dead. The entire precinct, which is marked off by a platform about three metres (ten feet) high, contains many pyramidal bases and sunken rectangular courts, all no doubt intended for various religious rituals.

Within the temple-site of the Citadel the most important and impressive building is a six-storeyed temple, which the Aztecs said was dedicated to the service of the god Quetzalcoatl. Since the various levels of the temple are all decorated with high relief carvings of serpents and demonic beings, as well as images of the god himself, we may have no reason to doubt the Aztecs. For all his fame as a god, there is much dispute as to the precise significance of the deity, even though it is certain that he was among the most important of the Oltec gods, even before he was adopted later by the Toltecs: he appears to have had many names and functions, the name by which we know him being given finally by the Aztecs.

In some ways the actual nature of this god has been misunderstood. The word *quetzl* means both 'bird' and 'precious', whilst *xolotl* means both 'serpent' and 'twin', and the latter name has been associated with the 'twin' Venus as both evening and morning planets, coming after and before the sun. The name refers more to the idea of a god 'emerging' from the feathered serpent, that is 'incarnating' into earthly form, than merely with the form itself. This is why in the finest images of the god we see the head of the god himself emerging from the serpent's mouth.

Generally it appears to be agreed that he was an air god, with many of the same attributes as the Mercury of the Romans, for he was protector of the arts, the teacher of all things beautiful, and the messenger between human beings and the higher gods. He was the Lord of Healing, and may also have been connected with the idea of redemption through death – yet it is clear that the Oltecs and the later Aztecs did not view death in quite the same way as we do in modern times. Death for them (as indeed with almost all ancient races) was a moment of transition, of liberation from the material plane which permitted the spirit to return unfettered to its true spiritual home. It is perhaps this view which allowed the sacrificial victims to participate so willingly in their own deaths. It has been suggested that the feathers of the plumage worn by this god Quetzalcoatl were particularly linked with this idea of spiritual redemption, for the bird was seen to live more in the world of spirit (that is, in the air) than upon the material level of the earth. It is tantalizing how little we ultimately know about the nature of this supremely important

god, who is reputed to have brought civilization to ancient Mexico and was the teacher of all things beautiful.

The Pyramid of the Sun is the dominating part of Teotihuacan's ceremonial centre. The visitor is still able to see this pyramid from any point during his walk along the strangely named Causeway Avenue, but of course the temple of the Moon appears and disappears as he ascends and descends the mounds which were originally paved steps. The stability of the first temple pyramid, contrasted with the illusory movement of the second, may well account for the choice of names given them by the Aztecs, for the actual movement of the sun and moon do exhibit these characteristics – the sun being regular and the moon erratic in its relatively rapid movement and its changing form during its phases.

The actual name Teotihuacan is derived from a Nahuatl word which means 'the place where one becomes a god'. This may relate to the idea of death according to the concept whereby every human being at death is taken into the spiritual world, and becomes like a god. But it could also be related to the idea of a spiritual liberation through religious or other disciplines. The single root word *teotia* around which the name is constructed actually means 'to worship', and it does seem that the main activity within this city was the worship of the gods. It had also, however, the more usual functions of a city, and was indeed the central market for a vast area around the mountainous regions which are now called Mexico. At the height of its power Teotihuacan appears to have had as many as 85,000 inhabitants.

One of the most lovely buildings in the city is the Palace of Quetzalpapalotl, once more with an Aztec name, who was a sort of butterfly-god. Since it was believed that butterflies were the outer forms of the spirits of the dead – an idea which was also widely accepted in many European cultures – it would seem that this spiritual being was connected with the state immediately after death, and, therefore, once more with that important body-free experience.

In contrast to this rather beautiful god, another widely-worshipped figure was that of Tlaloc, whose horrific image is still to be found in the wall paintings which survive. He was the god of rain, and was called *Chac* by the Maya. All in all, the physical remains of Teotihuacan survive as frustratingly intriguing hints as to the nature of the civilization that once stood here. Through the mystery in which they are shrouded we see evidence indeed of the work of giants, albeit only metaphorically.

Above left A mosaic-work funerary mask from Teotihuacan.
Above A painted terracotta mask from Teotihuacan.

Palenque

'In the romance of the world's history nothing ever impressed me more forcibly than the spectacle of this once great and lovely city, over-turned, desolate, and lost . . . overgrown with trees for miles around and without even a name to distinguish it.' So wrote the American explorer and archaeologist Stevens in adulation of his first view of the Mayan city of Palenque.

The chance meeting of Stevens – still described in our own century as 'the greatest of American travel writers' – and the English artist Catherwood in Leicester Square, London, led to a rediscovery and preparatory charting of the Mayan civilization, and marked the beginning of serious American archaeology. The two brought a much needed direction to the study of Mayan culture at a time when serious argument raged as to whether such hidden buildings (known now to be Olmec, Toltec and Mayan in origin) were to be traced to cultures as far apart in space and time as the Egyptians, the Norsemen, the Chinese, the Mongols (who were supposed to have come to the Americas with elephants), the Romans, the Phoenicians, and even the lost tribe of Israel – the latter idea, incidentally, not yet entirely dispelled by all the labours of modern archeologists!

This city 'without even a name' which the two men were to reveal to an astonished world was called Palenque, being derived from the Spanish for 'palisade'; even by the time of the Spanish conquest, however, the city had been lost and forgotten. It had been stumbled on, from time to time, by travellers, but it had never been systematically explored and recorded in the way envisaged by Stevens. Nowadays, almost certainly because of the impetus given by the studies and researches of this great American, the unknown Palenque, in the remote Chiapas region of Mexico, is described by one modern authority as 'perhaps the most famous, the most accessible, and the most visited' of Mayan sites.

When Stevens and his friend found it, however, it was scarcely recognizable as a complex of buildings, as it was entangled in a thousand years of forest growth. Eventually their work revealed the structure of a city as remarkable in its beauty as in its lost splendour. The main ruins still standing today are those of the Palace, and the three temples called by their modern names of 'the Three Tablets', 'the Cross' and 'the Sun'. The most elaborate is the Palace – which may in fact have been a religious centre as much as a palace. This stands upon an oblong stone mound (a Mayan 'pyramid') 12 metres (40 feet) high, and 93 by 78 metres (310 by 260 feet), which was almost certainly originally decorated with bright colours. The Palace on top is 9 metres (30 feet) high, and has dimensions of 54 by 68 metres (180 by 228 feet), with walls pierced by forty doorways. There are many corridors and rooms within the Palace, variously regarded, as the archaeologist Bancroft records, 'as sleeping rooms, dungeons, or sepulchres, according to the temperament of the observer'.

When Stevens and his companion reached the large building now called 'the Temple of the Inscriptions' (because of the 620 sculpted glyphs within it – one of the longest inscriptions in Mayan art) they stood in rapt silence, for the connection between this site and other Mayan centres began to dawn on them. Yet, even as they stood there, they were not to know that an even greater treasure lay beneath their feet.

In June 1952, while working in this Temple, the Mexican archaeologist Lhuillier observed on the floor, which was of course raised on the pyramidal base, a slab containing finger-holes. Naturally, he had this raised, and one might imagine his excitement when he discovered behind it a curving passageway which led to . . . a blockage of rubble and stones! Almost three years later, after much sweat and blood, Lhuillier was led to an

The temple-pyramid known as the 'Temple of the Cross' at Palenque.

154

underground crypt 'guarded' by the skeletal remains of six humans, one of whom had been a woman. Within the crypt was an extraordinary array of statues and rich objects, as well as a heavy stone sarcophagus which contained the body of some important personage, perhaps that of a priest-king. The dating within (expressed of course in Mayan glyphs) indicated that this secret room must have been used as a burial chamber in about AD 633. The discovery of this curious burial chamber changed the official view of the purpose behind the Mayan pyramidal temples, for since the chamber was some 2 metres (6 feet) below ground level, it was reasonably certain that the pyramid had been built afterwards, making this distinctly a combination of temple and funerary monument. As Lhuillier himself wrote, it was here that 'the most secret and important rites of

Temple of the Inscriptions. The pyramid foundation is unique in that it contains a scant burial chamber. The cross-section shows the internal stairway. An underground passage half way down lets in air and light.

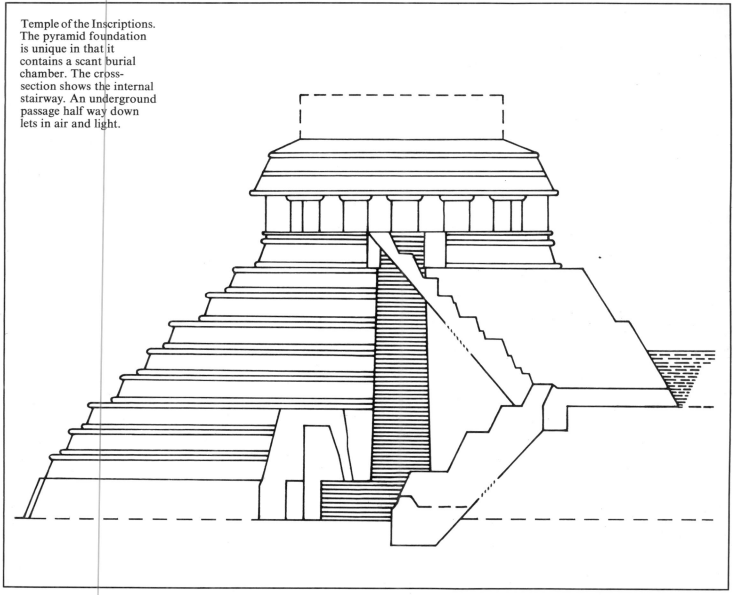

texts so frequently speak, and which was supposed to have occupied the area now called the Atlantic ocean thousands of years ago, but it is certain that the Egyptians did not influence the Mayans, as was suggested even fairly recently.

The saddest story of the lost city of Palenque is still to be told. The walls of the Palace, like all the other buildings, were probably originally covered in a fine stucco which was richly painted. However, some well-intentioned workers burned away much of the forest vegetation to clear the area for their studies, with the result that the plaster dried out and crumbled, and the paintings were destroyed – what nature had failed to do in twelve hundred years, men did in a few hours. The act of folly was a real tragedy for Palenque, since, due to a series of geological and weather conditions within the area, the stucco which under normal conditions would have easily crumbled, had been preserved. Now very few of the paintings remain, but those which do, alongside the painted records of such artists as Catherwood, are mute testimony to the high level of culture which existed in these regions of the Americas at a time when Europe was living in what have been called 'the Dark Ages'.

the Mayan religion were celebrated, probably involving human sacrifices'.

The neighbouring temple, called the Temple of the Cross by archaeologists, takes its name from the curious glyph within the building – a symbol which, as the historian von Hagen puts it, caused 'more learned controversy than any other piece of art in America' – a cross surrounded by purely Mayan symbols, such as the sacred bird *quetzal*. This 'cross' symbol provoked the priests who first heard about it to claim that the Mayan inhabitants of the region had been Christianized! The truth is, of course, that the cross in its many variant forms was a religious symbol in many widely dispersed cultures, such as India and Japan (not to mention Palestine) long before the advent of Christianity. There was as little point in drawing such a connection with the West, as in drawing a connection between the hieroglyphics of Egypt and these Mayan glyphs. Perhaps it is possible that these written forms did have a common ancestry in the written forms of the continent of Atlantis about which the occult

Above left Mayan image of a solar deity, found in the Temple of the Cross. *Left* Head of a sacrificed warrior from the crypt of the Temple of the Inscriptions.

Chichen Itza

The fantastic remains of Chichen Itza are a frustrating reminder that we know almost nothing about the Maya Indians who built it. It seems that the Itzas themselves were probably of Toltec origin, almost certainly one of the waves of invading tribes who overran the Yucatan, having been driven out of the Toltec Empire to the south when it collapsed in the late tenth century. They subdued those who lived here and established their capital at Chichen Itza, 185 kilometres (77 miles) southeast of the modern Merida. So little is known about these people that we are not even sure what they called themselves; the word 'Mayan' which we use is taken from the principal city of Mayapan, which developed after the fall of Chichen Itza. We do not even know why they did not make use of the wheel in their vast building enterprises, for they understood the principle, and how it could be used, for they put wheels on some of their children's toys. We know very little about their beliefs or religion, except that they involved complex sacrificial rituals. What we do know about them is derived almost entirely from the surviving architectural remains, and from the few archaeological finds which have been preserved in our museums.

They built roads much like the Romans – straight roadways which cut through swamps, desert and thick undergrowth alike, and we are certain that at one time there was a huge network of such roads throughout their territory. We may also be reasonably certain that Chichen Itza was one of their principal cities, for of all the surviving remains this appears to have been the most sacred of centres: there are signs of large numbers of temples throughout the region, and it is said that even to this day there exist many ruins which are not yet known to modern man.

It is an impressive place, even in its ruin, for the massive pyramidal temple may be seen dominating the plain for some distance around. The centre had been old even when the invading Toltecs took over, but they brought with them much which was new and unknown in the area, including copper and gold. Among their more bizarre introductions were the rather sinister *Chac Mool* figures, recumbent statues with strange 'umbilical ashtrays', into which the freshly torn-out hearts of sacrificial victims were dropped as food for the gods.

Even the modern name of Chichen Itza is probably derived from such sacrificial rituals, for its name means 'mouth of the well of the Itza', and almost certainly refers to one of the wells near the city. This well is actually one of two, a more innocent one being reserved for ordinary water supplies, while this was used for ritual sacrifice on a grand scale. From one of the large temple squares there led a 9-metre (30-foot) wide ceremonial causeway a distance of some 270 metres (900 feet) to this snake-infested *cenote*, which is now heavily silted. Recent archaeological surveys have unearthed the skeletal remains of over four hundred sacrificial victims – very many of them children – along with many artefacts and treasures. The well is very large, about 56 metres (186 feet) in average diameter, and about 35 metres (116 feet) from the top of the precipice to its deepest point. It appears to have been the centre of some curious propitiatory rituals, the secrets of which have been entirely lost – though of course there is no lack of inspired guesswork as to their nature.

The site of Chichen Itza is fortunately well preserved, and has been well restored, with the result that, although it is a centre of tourism it retains its eerie beauty. The most important buildings are the pyramid-temple, the Temple of the Warriors, the colonnade of the so-called 'thousand columns', the *caracol*, which is supposed to be an observatory, and a ball-game court within the temple precinct. Each of these buildings is worth attention.

The serpent columns of
the Temple of the
Warriors.

The temple of Kukulkan (a Toltec name for the same god known to the Aztecs as Quetzalcoatl), was called by the conquering Spaniards the Pyramid *del Castillo* because their leaders established this as a fortress headquarters during their bloody conquest of the area. They had heavy cannons hauled to the top of the pyramidal support, in order to dominate the area with their firepower. This enormous terraced pyramid is 23 metres (78 feet) high, and rests on a square base with sides nearly 54 metres (180 feet) in length. It is generally believed that the nine terraces of this pyramidal support are intended to symbolize the nine regions of the Mayan underworld (the equivalent of our purgatory), and the 365 steps of the four great stairways correspond to the days in the civil year.

Kukulkan, depicted throughout Central American Indian culture as a plumed serpent, was the god of the winds. As such he was the messenger of the higher gods, and made available to man the knowledge of science and crafts. His status as revealer of learning can perhaps be gauged from the careful planning with which the buildings dedicated to him must have been constructed.

The temple on top of the truncated pyramid is, along with its support, orientated to the four cardinal points, and is reached by means of four great stairways which have a continuous balustrade with the plumed serpent motif. While the temple itself is a simple box form (which would have been coated in stucco, and brightly painted), there is now an open access to early pyramidal remains within the body of the present structure. This 'hidden pyramid' is an interesting survival, for under normal circumstances the older forms were destroyed entirely in order to make way for new buildings. It has been suggested, with a fair degree of certainty, that the Aztecs and the Toltecs built according to a

View towards the 'thousand columns' surrounding the Temple of the Warriors.

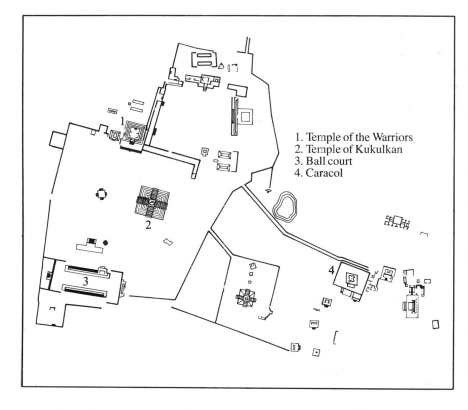

Plan of the city.

kind, 6·6 metres (22 feet) in diameter and 7·2 metres (24 feet) tall, with two narrow corridors running around a solid masonry core. The structure rests upon a double truncated pyramid, the upper one measuring 16·5 by 24 metres (55 by 80 feet), the lower one 45 by 67 metres (150 by 223 feet).

Within the temple precinct is the ball-game court, 81 by 7·5 metres (270 by 25 feet), where the Mayans and the later Toltecs played *tlachtli,* a fast and furious game, apparently something like modern basketball. It was played between two groups of men who were forbidden by the rules to touch the rubber ball with feet or hands, but had to use their hips, elbows and heads to keep it off the ground. It seems that the aim of the game was to score by driving the ball through a small hole in the stonework, high above the heads of the players – a feat which must have required great skill. It is evident that the game was permeated throughout with a strong religious element, which explains the location of the ball-court within the religious precinct. Some historians have suggested that there is some evidence for believing that the losing team (or perhaps the captain of that team) was sacrificed at the end of the game. Others have suggested, however, that such was the attitude to sacrifice among these people that it would be the winning team who would merit such a 'reward'!

It is possible that the ball game is in some way linked with the legends of the Popol Vuh, one of the ancient texts consisting of a collection of legends. The story goes that one of the different races of men made by the gods (which included the mindless men of clay, and the soulless wooden men), rebelled against the gods. One outcome of this was that the 'heavenly twins', Hunhunapu (god of the hunt) and Ixbalanque (the little jaguar) descended into the underworld of Xibalba in order to avenge the death of their father, who had been killed in the ensuing war. This curious vengeance involved a mystic ball game, and finally the eviction of the inhabitants from their native Xibalba. The link with the 'real' game of tlachtli may be involved with this curious myth, as it appears that the Mayan Empire was at one time called 'Xibalba', as though the Mayans themselves were identified with the outcasts from the underworld realms.

religious calendar scheme, with a periodicity of fifty-two years, a period which marked the recurrent union of the civil and religious calendrical systems.

To the east of the Spanish fortress can be seen the so-called 'thousand columns': quadruple rows of pillars which encircle the Temple of the Warriors. They are composed of overlaid cylindrical sections with square plinths on top. There are 380 of these pillars, now measuring 1–2 metres (3–6 feet) in height. The Temple of the Warriors takes its name from relief carvings on these surrounding columns of beautifully worked images of armed spearmen, with helmets and armour. The huge pillars marking the entrance to the temple are ornately worked figures of the plumed serpent, whose fanged gaping mouths rest upon the earth, and whose raised plumed tails support the huge lintels. All the columns and the serpent and warrior decorations would have been painted with vivid, if not garish, colours. It is estimated that the temple was built round about AD 1100. In spite of its name, the purpose of the building is obscure.

The caracol is another building with an obscure purpose, though it has been suggested that it was an observatory from which priests studied the movements of the planets, and made calendrical calculations. It is a circular and domed building, unique of its

Tenochtitlan

'Gazing at such wonderful sights, we did not know what to say, or whether what appeared before us was real,' wrote the Spaniard Bernard Diaz del Castillo, one of the soldiers of Cortes, when he saw for the first time the miraculous city of Tenochtitlan.

It was a fairyland city, built upon an island on the edge of a lake, joined to the mainland by a series of raised carriageways, surrounded by artificial floating gardens, with canal waterways within it, and whole gardens of plants, shrubs and trees everywhere among the richly decorated buildings. After the hard trek through the wilderness of mountains and plains, no wonder Diaz and his companions believed they were in a dream: 'It is like the enchantments they tell of in the legends of Amadis. Are not the things we see a dream?'

Curiously enough, the city had begun quite literally as a dream. Early in the fourteenth century, a priest of the Aztec communities which had recently been driven by warring tribes from their homeland had a dream in which the humming-bird of war appeared and told him how he would be able to identify a new site, where the Aztecs would be able to build a city 'which would be queen and lady of all the others of the earth'. This city was to be the mighty Tenochtitlan.

The earliest map we have of this city is one which was drawn by a surveyor from among the soldiers of Cortes. They eventually destroyed the place and a vast number of the inhabitants, whom Cortes had reduced to utter famine through a seventy-five-day siege, which resulted in sights which made even him sick. The map shows the circular city of Tenochtitlan covering the island in the western part of what was then Lake Lexoco. It reveals a unique Aztec city, and indeed one of the most remarkable in the world: no known city was then of such a vast size. It was said that the number of people living in this island-city, when the rule of their King

Montezuma was at its height (around AD 1510) was over 300,000. Perhaps this is not a high figure by modern standards, but by way of comparison we might take the population of Florence, in Italy, at that time, which was only 135,000, even before it was ravaged by the plague, and yet Florence was listed as one of the great cities in Europe. It is further recorded that Montezuma had so extended the territories around (mainly to gain tribute and prisoners for the bloody Aztec cult of human sacrifice to the gods) that by 1519 he had rule over an empire of five million souls in central and southern Mexico, for whom this city was the capital.

Virtually nothing now remains of this once magnificent city, which was perhaps at one time the greatest in the world. Cortes and his men made quite sure of this, for they pulled down the houses, palaces and temples, of which there were supposed to be 360 in this city – 'as many as the year has days' as the Aztec guides explained. Over the ruins they laid the foundations of the modern Mexico City. The chief surviving element from this ruthless, and indeed quite thoughtless and unnecessary, Spanish devastation, is the grid-system city plan, and there are a few other echoes: the Colonial plaza is laid over the old Aztec market, for example, and the cathedral is situated near the former site of the main temple of the Aztecs, whilst the location of the National Palace is over one of those belonging to Montezuma, and so on. However, only a reconstruction can give an idea of the vanished magnificence of this ancient city.

According to the accounts of Cortes himself, the wide streets were made half of stones and earth, and half of water, so that the Aztecs might either walk or canoe. These canal-streets were spanned by massive and beautiful bridges. All the streets led to the centre of the island, where there was a sacred precinct, a huge square enclosing a

Sculpture of Coatlicue, the Earth Mother, excavated from beneath the cathedral square of Mexico City, where it had been buried after the total destruction of Tenochtitlan by the Spaniards.

TENOCHTITLAN

The main religious precinct of Tenochtitlan as it would have been seen by the Spaniards under Cortes. Cortes himself left a detailed account of the appearance of these 'idol houses' which has contributed to the ideas expressed in their reconstruction. He tells how the walls were made of polished stone and carved woodwork, and were decorated with monsters and strange figures. 'From the main temple narrow doorways lead to small chapels, where smaller idols stand. Those rooms were all full of human blood which had spilled over during the sacrifices.'

The dual-temple pyramid which dominated the area was dedicated to the Aztec god of war (Huitzilopochtli) and the rain god (Tlaloc). Like all religious centres, the buildings in the precinct were intended to serve the complex rituals of sacrifice and propitiation ceremonies, and to house the large number of priests and administrators, at a time when there was no strict dividing line between the priesthood and political administration.

This entire area was destroyed by the Spaniards in the early decades of the sixteenth century, and the Cathedral of Mexico City now stands over this particular precinct.

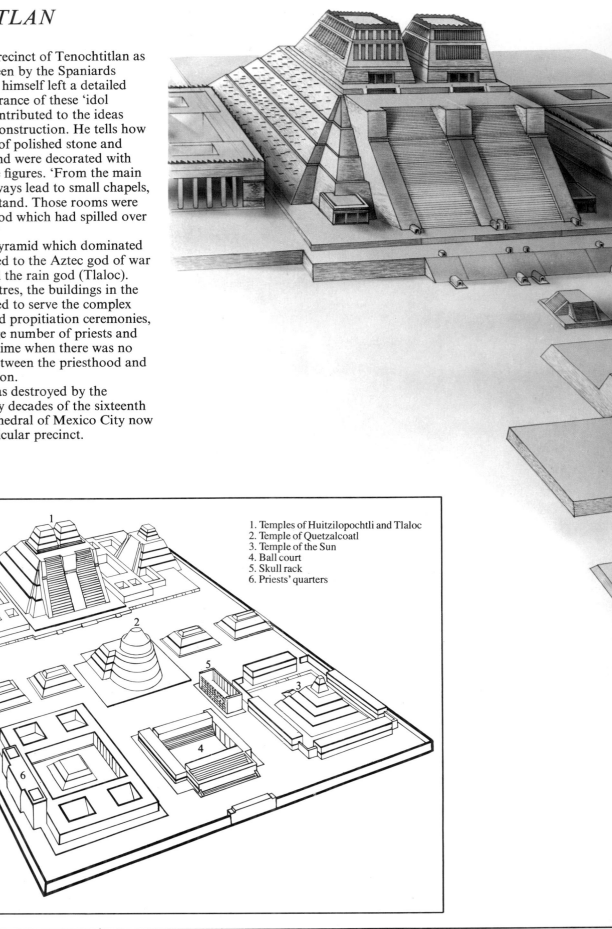

1. Temples of Huitzilopochtli and Tlaloc
2. Temple of Quetzalcoatl
3. Temple of the Sun
4. Ball court
5. Skull rack
6. Priests' quarters

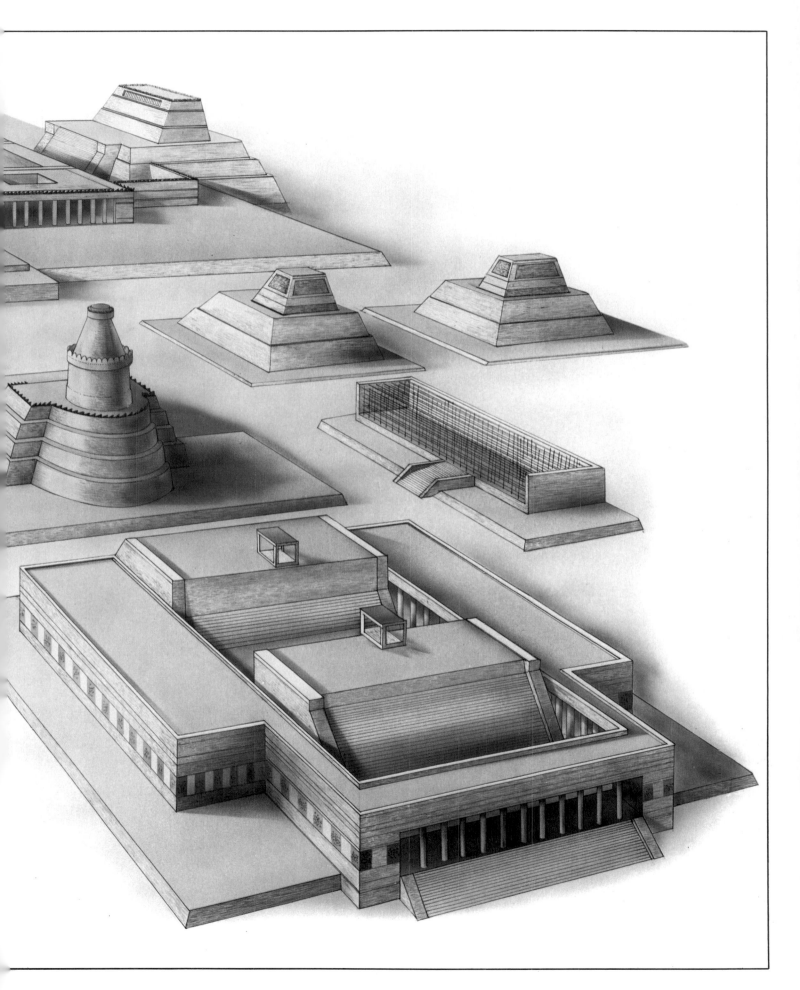

whole series of buildings designed to serve a variety of religious functions, around which Aztec life was organized. The area of this precinct was that of a square with walls 420 metres (1400 feet) long, but this surrounding wall was no ordinary partition, for it was intricately decorated with the heads of the plumed serpents which figured so largely in the religious cults of the Aztecs – not surprisingly, this structure was called the Serpent Wall.

Dominating this large religious precinct was a great pyramid which, from its height of 30 metres (97 feet), supported two temples, one of which was dedicated to the Aztec god of War (Huitzilopochtli), which was painted red, the other being dedicated to the rain god Tlaloc, and was painted blue. Some distance

from this twin temple was the circular temple of Quetzalcoatl, the 'plumed serpent', supported by a broad base, its entrance marked by the gaping fangs of a gigantic serpent. From this temple door a priest would twice a day beat an enormous drum, which would resound throughout the city, marking the beginning and end of the day's work. Beyond was another huge pyramid, resting on a base 100 by 80 metres (330 by 264 feet), which appears to have been dedicated to the Sun-god.

Also within the precinct was a magnificent ball court where the game of *tlachtli* would have been played. This was a game somewhat like the modern game of basketball, played at considerable pace. The players were required to project the ball through a

The largely reconstructed Aztec temple at modern Santa Cecilia near the ancient site of Tenochtitlan.

Right Giant stone 'calendar' which originally stood on a platform half-way up the great pyramid at Tenochtitlan. To the left of it a detail showing the heads of the great serpents which symbolize time.

small hole high up in the wall. What made the game especially difficult was the rule that they were not allowed to touch the ball with their hands or their feet, but had to use their heads, their elbows, or their hips. Tlachtli was a very popular game with the Aztecs, but, unlike modern sports, its nature and significance appear to have been deeply religious.

Near to the ball court was the skull-rack, where the flesh-stripped heads of sacrificed victims were strung together in a permanent ghastly exhibition. Not far from this was a circular stone which marked the centre of gladiatorial sacrifices. Here, on certain ceremonial days, a tethered prisoner was set to defend himself with a simple club against a trained adversary who had a club mounted with razor-sharp knife blades.

The Aztec ceremonies of human sacrifice have been described many times, and a multitude of pictures have survived which convey to us the outer forms of these quite awful bloody rituals. The sacrificial victim (who, strange to tell, appears to have participated in the ritual with as much dignity and willingness as those around him) was divested of his ceremonial robes, and then was held naked, with his back over a huge stone, by four men, each holding a limb. In this uncomfortable posture, his rib-cage was arched high, and the priest, or at times the king, who was also a priest, could cut deeply into the chest beneath the rib cage and stomach with a sharp obsidian knife, and then tear out the palpitating heart of the victim. This bloody heart would then be placed on a special altar, and dedicated to one of the gods, after which it was burned. At the more spectacular rituals, as many as 20,000 victims would be sacrificed at the same time in this terrible way.

It is a relief to turn away from such practices to the few surviving works of art made by these curious people. Perhaps the most famous of such works from this particular city is the huge Calendar Stone, covered in hieroglyphics which tell the story of the Aztec world, within a framework of days and years. This stone calendar was made around 1470 under the rule of King Axayacatl, the predecessor of Montezuma: it weighs over 20 tonnes, and is 4 metres (13 feet) in diameter. Since the Aztec used neither wheel nor beast of burden, we must assume that this vast stone was pulled on wooden rollers from the mainland by human beings. In the centre of the stone is carved in an image of the Sun-god Tonatiuh, and around him hieroglyphics which give the dates of the four previous ages of the world. It seems that the Aztecs believed that they were living in the fifth epoch, and that while the people of the last epoch were destroyed by Water, the people of this present fifth age will be destroyed by Earthquakes. On the periphery of the circle are the images of two fire serpents, which are thought to symbolize the idea of time – a symbolism surprisingly similar to that adopted in some European cultures, which use the image of a snake biting its own tail to represent the idea of eternity.

Machu Picchu

Probably the quickest and most unlikely coup in military history occurred in November 1532, when the Spaniard Pizarro seized the Inca King Atahualpa from among his 30,000 soldier guards, and by this act began the conquest of a whole Empire of some three million by a mere 170 men.

Even as the galleon of treasure arrived in Seville, bearing the million-pound ransom of the Inca king – the richest and most beautiful collection of gold and silver ever seen in one place, the entire treasure of the Incas – and even while Spain marvelled at the beauty of the objects, in that other New Continent, the last of the great South American kingdoms of the Sun was being raped and mutilated. Indeed, it was already in its last death throes, and their King Atahuallpa was being strangled.

The devastation was thorough and efficient. Round about 1500, at the height of its power, the Empire of the Incas had spread from the Sun temples of Purumauca in southern Chile to the Ancasmayo in modern Colombia, a distance of over 4800 kilometres (3600 miles). It had good roads, and efficient religious and administrative systems – altogether it was a civilization which rivalled that of Rome at its peak. Within a few years this bright Inca world had set in a sea of blood, its golden works of art melted down in the Spanish foundries.

And yet, from the remains of a relatively small but spectacular Inca site on the Urubamba gorge, we may catch a glimpse of this vanished splendour. In Machu Picchu – although it housed as few as 1200 people – a whole galaxy of temples, plazas, and administrative centres stand as mute testimony to what has been lost.

This Inca village overlooks the Urubamba river from a dizzy height of 900 metres (3000 feet). It is now without doubt one of the most visited of all Inca ruins, but in fact this tends to convey an erroneous picture of Inca life.

The Inca Empire excelled in the building of planned cities, centred upon religious functions, yet the real wonder of Machu Picchu lies not so much in its architectural planning as in its siting, perched as it is, almost precariously on a large precipice, surrounded on three sides by a deep canyon. It was to this deserted and forgotten site that Hiram Bingham of Yale University made his way during his search for the lost cities of the Incas, and later wrote of these 'ruins of what we now believe was the lost city of Vicapampa the Old, perched on top of a narrow ridge lying below the peak of Machu Picchu, [now] called the ruins of Machu Picchu because when we found them no one knew what else to call them'.

This town is part of a chain of loosely connected hill fortresses probably designed to defend the Inca city of Cuzco, where Pizarro met his death in 1541. Two walls, about 250 metres (800 feet) apart, protect the town to the south (the only conceivable side open to attack). The centre of the town is dominated by a long stairway, the 'Stairs of the Fountains', a so-called Royal Mausoleum, and a semicircular temple. It was a very well-preserved town, in its virtually inaccessible perch, which Professor Bingham discovered in 1911. Apparently it had been deserted *en masse* by its inhabitants, and was unknown to the Spaniards, which is presumably why it has survived intact. There is reason to suppose that it was built in the last half of the fifteenth century. Besides the usual complement of temples, shrines and houses, the town has an extremely elaborate series of stone water basins, as well as a large number of stone staircases – over a hundred were counted by Bingham in the area of the central citadel alone – a demand made of the builders by the uneven terrain upon which the town was perched.

On the summit of the western hill, to the north of the series of plazas and terraces upon

Aerial view of the mountain city of Machu Picchu.

which the Incas grew their corn, tomatoes and potatoes, stood a small temple. It was built around the 'sundial stone', the *intihuatana*, which is supposed to have been the pillar to which the priests symbolically tied the sun in order to stop it disappearing, which would have meant the end of mankind. This pillar is actually an enormous monolith, cut to the form of a trapezoidal prism, which rests upon a square base.

Machu Picchu must have been an extraordinary place to live, yet by Inca standards the town was probably not all that special. Its survival and surprising condition has none the less led some modern writers to see a secret meaning in its design and placing, but such suggestions show only how speculative is our understanding of the Incas.

GLOSSARY

ACROPOLIS Greek word meaning 'upper city'. The chief temples and treasuries of ancient cities were built like citadels on hills.

ADYTON The sacred room, especially within a Greek temple, although the word is also applied to the sacred room in Egyptian temples.

AGORA The Greek equivalent of the Latin *Forum*.

AMPHITHEATRE Term derived from the Greek, meaning 'double theatre' (Greek theatres being semi-circular). An oval or circular building with seats arranged in tiers around and above the central *Arena*.

AMPODYTERIUM Greek name for the dressing room in bath-houses.

APSE Originally a Latin name for the circular or angular end of a *Basilica*; later applied to the same in Christian churches.

ARENA The Latin for 'sand', hence the central area of an *Amphitheatre*, originally. Now often applied to the entire building.

ATRIUM An entrance hall, open to the sky, much like a courtyard, in a Roman house.

BASILICA In Roman times, a huge hall used mainly as a court of Justice – in Christian times such halls were adopted for worship, and hence the term was applied to a special design of church.

CALIDARIUM The hot-water room within a Roman bath-house.

CARYATIDS Stone or marble figures of females used in architecture as columns or supports.

CHAITYA Buddhist term for a 'meeting hall'.

COMPOSITE ORDER Sometimes called the 'Roman' *Order* – an architectural unit combining elements of the *Ionic* and the *Corinthian*. It is highly decorative.

CORINTHIAN ORDER An *Order* with a bell-shaped capital, from which emerge eight acanthus stalks, supporting the *Volutes*.

CUPOLA A spherical roof, much like an inverted cup, from the Latin word *cupa*, meaning 'cup'.

DAGOBA A Sanskrit term for a sacred mound or tower, intended to house Buddhist relics. The equivalent of *Stupa*.

DORIC ORDER An *Order* with a plain capital, a fluted shaft, and with no base to the column.

DROMOS A narrow, uncovered passageway, leading to an underground tomb.

ENTASIS Greek term used now in architecture to indicate the outer swelling of a column, intended to subtly counteract the effect of ordinary vision which makes a straight column appear to curve inwards.

FORUM A public open space within a Roman civic centre, intended for both social and market purposes.

FRESCO In general, any wall painting. In its original meaning (Italian for 'fresh'), it was used for painting done into still-wet plaster on the wall, which subsequently dried within the surface of the plaster.

FRIGIDARIUM The cold water room within a Roman bath-house.

GLYPH From the Greek word meaning 'groove', a symbol or design carved into a smooth surface. But see also *Hieroglyphic*.

HIEROGLYPHIC From the Greek meaning 'sacred' (*hieros*) and *Glyph*. Applied originally to Egyptian sacred writings incised in stone, then to ordinary written sacred writings on paper. Applied now to any sacred writings in non-alphabetic languages.

HYPOSTYLE A combination of Greek (*hypo*, 'under') and Latin (*stylus*, 'pillar'), meaning a pillared hall which is completely or partly roofed.

IONIC ORDER An *Order* which is almost an elegant and refined *Doric*, with slim columns, often fluted, and refined, tightly wound *Volutes*.

MURAL Term derived from the Latin originally relating only to the idea of a 'wall', but eventually limited to wall paintings. Such paintings could be in the technique of *Fresco* or *Tempera*, but in modern times may be in oil or polymer paints.

NAOS Greek word meaning 'dwelling', applied to the main room in a temple, which was the dwelling place of the god, usually containing a statue of that god.

NAUMACHIA Greek word meaning 'naval battle', but used mainly of staged sea fights in *amphitheatres*.

NAVE Word traced by some to the Latin *Navis*, 'ship', by others to the Greek *Naos*, 'dwelling', being the central aisle of the church building, in contrast to the side aisles.

NECROPOLIS Greek word meaning 'city of the dead' – a funerary area.

NIRVANA Sanskrit word meaning 'freedom from animal desires and from the trammels of the material world's illusion'. This is a high state of bliss.

OBELISK A high pillar (usually of marble or stone) of tapering square section, terminating in a pyramid.

OMPHALOS Greek word meaning 'navel'. Used specifically to refer to a large shaped stone at Delphi which marks the supposed centre of the world.

ORDERS In architecture, an order consists of the shaft of a column, usually standing on a base, and its capital, the decorated top portion supporting an entablature. There were three Greek orders – the *Doric, Ionic* and *Corinthian*. But see also *Composite*.

PERISTYLE A row or series of rows of columns around a courtyard or temple.

PIAZZA Italian word for 'public square'.

PRECOLUMBIAN A name applied to those cultures in the Southern Americas prior to the arrival of Columbus in the late fifteenth century.

PROPYLAEUM Greek word meaning 'entrance portal', and applied to the imposing gateways before the sacred enclosures or *Temenos*.

PYLON Greek word meaning 'gateway', and applied especially to the monumental masses of masonry before Egyptian temples.

ROTUNDA A round building.

SARCOPHAGUS A coffin, usually richly carved and in some permanent material, such as marble.

SIKHARA The conical or pyramidial 'spire' above a Hindu shrine.

STUPA A mound-like monument, usually of complex symbolic structure, dedicated to the Buddha.

SUDATORIUM The sweat-room in a Roman bath-house.

SUTRA Sanskrit word applied to Buddhist sacred literary discourses.

TEMENOS Greek word applied to the sacred area in which was located a temple or sanctuary.

TEMPERA A technique of painting in which the colours are made to adhere to the surface (very often a wall-surface) by means of egg-yolk or egg-white.

TEPIDARIUM The warm-water rooms in the Roman bath-house.

TLACHTLI A fast ball-game with religious overtones, played by several Precolumbian cultures.

TORANA A gateway, intended largely for ceremonial use, and of a complex symbolic nature, before a single Buddhist *Stupa*.

UNCTUARIUM A room in the Roman bath-house used especially for oiling and annointing.

VELARIUM A huge 'sail' or protective covering which could be unfurled above a theatre or amphitheatre to protect spectators.

VOLUTE The spiral capitals used in the *Orders*, from the latin word *voluta*, meaning 'scroll'.

ZIGGURAT A pyramidal tower built in steps, the central unit of Mesopotamian temple complexes.

BIBLIOGRAPHY

Ashley, M., *The Seven Wonders of the World*, London 1979

Audric, J., *Angkor and the Khmer Empire*, London 1972

Banks, E. J., *The Seven Wonders of the Ancient World*, London 1916

Baumann, H., *The Land of Ur*, London and New York 1969

Birley, A., *Septimius Severus*, London 1971

Ceram, C. W., *Gods, Graves and Scholars*, London 1971

Cottrell, L., *Lost Cities*, London and New York 1963

Cottrell, L., *Egypt*, London and New York 1966

Ediger, D., *The Well of Sacrifice: The Recovery of the Lost Mayan Treasures of Chichen Itza*, London 1971

Edwards, I. E. S., *The Treasures of Tutankhamun*, London and New York 1976

Fletcher, B., *A History of Architecture* (18th edn), London and New York 1975

Furneaux, R., *Ancient Mysteries*, London 1976, New York 1977

Greene, F., *Peking*, London and New York 1978

Hardoy, J. E., *Pre-Columbian Cities*, London 1973

Helfritz, H., *Mexican Cities of the Gods*, New York 1968

Huxley, J., *From an Antique Land*, New York 1954

Ivanoff, P., *Maya*, London and New York 1973

Kazantzakis, N., *Travels in China and Japan*, London and New York 1964

Kirkup, J., *Japan Behind the Fan*, London 1970

Macaulay, R., *Pleasure of Ruins*, London 1953

Menen, A., *Cities in the Sand*, London 1972

Perowne, S., *The Archaeology of Greece and the Aegean*, London 1974

Trevelyan, R., *The Shadow of Vesuvius: Pompeii AD 79*, London 1976, New York 1977

Von Hagen, V., *Search for the Maya: The Story of Stephens and Catherwood*, New York 1973

Woolley, C. L., *Excavations at Ur*, London and Scranton, Pa, n.d.

ACKNOWLEDGMENTS

We are grateful to the following for the use of photographs: BBC Hulton Picture Library 13; J. Allan Cash Limited 108/9; Werner Forman Archive 126/7, 130/31, 148/9, 150/51, 158/9, 160, 163, 166; F. Gigon 140; Sonia Halliday Photographs 42/3, 63, 98/9; Robert Harding Associates: R. Cundy 155, C. Gascoigne 112, 119, 121, 137, Hackforth-Jones 30, 41 bottom, R. Harding title page, D. Harissiadis 1, 65; V. Kennett 105, J. Ross 31, John Hillelson Agency: Dr G. Gerster 44/5; Michael Holford Library 47; I.G.D.A.: 90, 91, 133, 145, 157, 168/9, Archivio B 76, 77, Bertinetti 122/3, 129, Bevilacqua 24, 33, 67, 72, 73, 74/5, 82, 83, 84/5, 89, Borromeo 96, 115, Ciccione 46, Cirani 21, 39, 53, 101, 103, 106, 111, 156, Dagli Orti 18/19, 23, 25, 27, 36/7, 40 top, 49, 51, 52, 120, 152, 153, De Antonis 86/7, Di Francecantonio 66, Nimatallah 62, 71, P 2, 125, Prato 132, Pubbliaerfoto 61, 88, 93, Stournaras 64; Japan Information Centre, London 147; M. Leigheb 142, 143; The Mansell Collection 8, 10, 12, 14, 16, 17; Orbis 35; M. Pell-Lenars 139; Scala 58/9; S.E.F. 97; ZEFA 28/9, 50, 68/9, 80/81, 94/5, 116/17, 124, 130/31, 141.

Colour illustrations by Kevin Maddison 54/5, 164/5; Gerald Whitcomb 78/9.

Line drawings by Peter Nicholls.

INDEX